America's Horses *and* Ponies

America's Horses *and* Ponies

written and illustrated by IRENE BRADY

HOUGHTON MIFFLIN COMPANY BOSTON

ACKNOWLEDGMENTS

MY SPECIAL THANKS go to the following people: Dion A. Albach, Verne Albright, Mrs. J. Barker, Jr., Mrs. Holly Carell, Art and Nancy Cooley, Miss Diane Fitzgerald, Mrs. Harold Franz, Dale Gossett, Mr. A. Howard Hasbrook, Miss Judith Hassed, George Hatley, Seth P. Holcombe, Gene Holter, Mrs. F. G. Johns, Miss Patricia Jones, Lavon Lichtenberger, Mrs. Rosalie MacWilliam, Alvin M. Mavis, Mrs. Jean Murdock, King Parsons, Ken and Marge Raasch, Mrs. Bruce Read, Richard Robinson, Ray Smiley, Elmer Smith, Mrs. Sidney Swett, Mrs. Ruth Thompson, Mrs. Karene Topp, Miss Bonnie Trent, Frank Turley, and Mr. C. Williamson. My profound apologies are extended to anyone whom I may inadvertently have missed.

I would also like to thank Professor Brian Patterson, who constructively criticized the prehistoric horse reconstructions; the librarians at the Carnegie Public Libraries in both Hood River, Oregon, and Caldwell, Idaho, for their unstinting helpfulness; my family, who gave constant encouragement and help; my sister Di, who prodded me diligently when I flagged; Lucas, who never criticized; and my husband Larry Kistler, without whose unfailing help I could never have finished this book.

Of course, the final responsibility for accuracy in both the text and illustrations lies with the author.

TABLE OF CONTENTS

for
LARRY
who cooked
suppers

Preface

THIS IS A book for curious people — for people who want to know the why, what, where, when, and how about horses. It does not say anything about methods of riding, matters of stable management, and horse-show etiquette, because these by themselves would fill a large volume.

But it does give a fairly complete picture of the thirty-eight most popular breeds of horses and ponies in the United States. In addition, it discusses the donkey and mule, the zebras we see in zoos, and the often disputed progenitors of modern horse — Przewalski's Horse and the rebred Tarpan — and how they evolved in the dim past from eohippus, the Dawn Horse.

The horses, ponies, and other equines shown in this book were chosen for several reasons. Those breeds which are well established and have registries in this country are naturally included, as are those breeds which have been recently imported and are showing substantial increases in numbers and popularity. Draft breeds are shown not for the above reasons, but because they have played such an important role in our country's formation, and because they are still often to be seen in exhibitions and at fairs. Zoo animals, the asses, and the prehistoric horses are included to give a rounded view of the horse and its closest relatives and ancestors. Some breeds are not included because their registries have ceased operation for one reason or another, or because they do not seem to be distinctly different from some other breed.

All the drawings are done to scale, so that each animal may be compared with every other animal in the book to find relative size and conformation. An attempt has been made, within the limitations of the pencil drawing, to show various coat patterns and markings found on horses. All the Appaloosa patterns are shown, as well as both types of pinto markings. Dapple, roan, and buckskin are also portrayed.

The need for such a book as this becomes apparent to anyone who tries to find information and pictures of all the horses and ponies found in this country, and relationships between and among them and their various wild relatives. This book is a compilation of information from well over a hundred sources, including books, magazines, personal correspondence, and question-answer sessions between the author and horsemen. Perhaps the best source, both as a magazine and correspondent, has been the *Western Horseman*.

Most breed registries were very helpful, and many registry secretaries, horse owners, and friends paid special attention to my needs and volunteered abundant information and suggestions.

1

Introduction

THE HORSE IS an American, first, last, and we may hope always. In the not too distant past, the culture and industry of this country and much of the world rested on the strong shoulders of the horse. Without the horse there could have been scarcely any transportation of goods except by water or slow, slow oxen. Without the horse, man was afoot unless he had a boat and could get where he was going by water. Without the horse, wheels didn't turn, machines didn't grind and roll, goods could not be produced — unless it could be done with water power. In fact, one might say that water and horses were once the two most important commodities of an expanding community. Where there was no water, men were considerably hampered unless they could obtain horses. That is how our country began — with horsepower — and although electricity has ousted horses from most tasks, we can still find a surprising portion of the population riding them.

Although sometimes used in a working capacity, they are usually ridden for pleasure these days by people of all ages. Girls seem to be in the majority, but thousands of young people, girls and boys, have formed 4-H Clubs with planned horse-oriented activities and sessions on riding methods and styles and the care and selection of the horse. This book is for them.

The usefulness of any horse is determined by many things: its age, its sex, its faults or good points of conformation, and sometimes the gaits it can perform. Perhaps a brief discussion of age and sex are in order.

To begin with, a newborn foal is called a colt if male and a filly if female. When it reaches four years of age, a colt becomes a stallion, and the filly a mare. A gelding (pronounced with a hard g) is a colt which has been castrated before it reaches maturity.

All horses pictured in this book are stallions because breed standards are formed for stallions, not mares. The mare of a given breed will have most of the conformation traits of the stallion except for these important points:

1) her neck is slimmer and not as crested, and her build in general is lighter than the stallion's.

2) her loin is slacker; often a mare which has foaled several times will be potty, but this has no bearing on her conformation as a whole.

3) she is broader and higher in the rear than a stallion, having more room internally for bearing young.

4) a mare with good breeding should show a subtle female fineness of quality in her facial molding. Though the uninitiated scoff at the idea, a horse-show judge will place a more feminine-looking mare higher than one with a less feminine face, all other things being equal.

A gelding is sometimes mistaken for a filly or mare at a casual glance, for sexual growth is affected by altering. If the animal is gelded early in life, it will not fill out like a stallion, and particularly will not have the arched heavy neck and powerful muscling of a stallion. If, on the other hand, it is gelded just before it reaches full maturity, it will remain at whatever stage of maturity it has reached. If gelded too late, there is the drawback that although its function as a stud will be ended, it will still have the

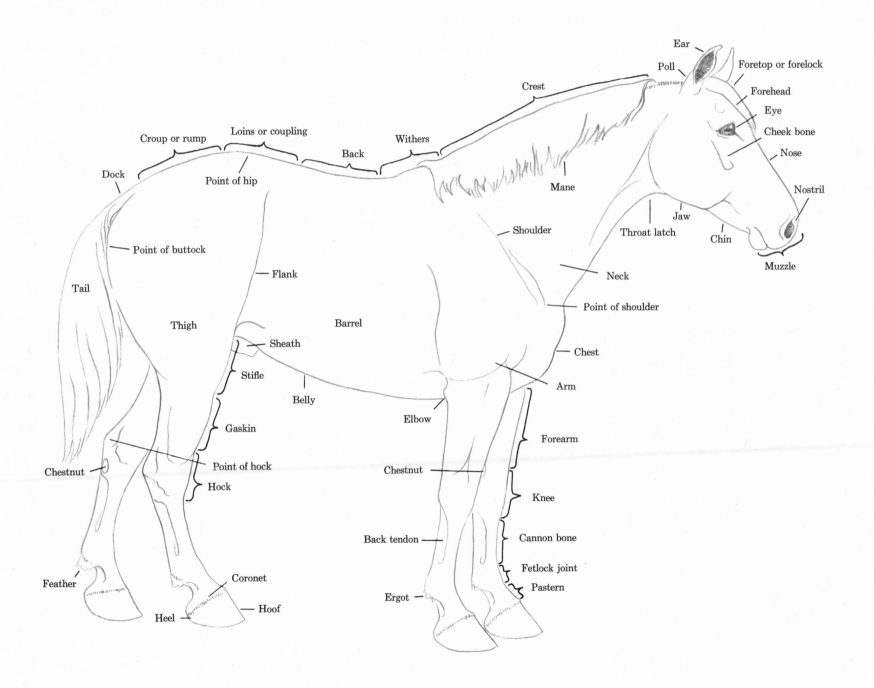

character and temperament of a stallion (often not as tractable and docile as one would wish).

Within this framework of age and sex, a horse of any given breed should have a good share of the conformation points or traits of the breed to which it belongs. However, a horse which is not of any particular breed may have as many good points of conformation as a purebred horse. The word "purebred" is often confused with the word "Thoroughbred," but a Thoroughbred is the race horse only, while the word "purebred" may apply to any animal, horse, dog, cat or mouse, which has impeccable breeding or a pedigree.

A diagram showing the parts of the horse is shown on page 3.

Color is an important factor among horse breeders and registries. Some registries are built around color or patterns — the Appaloosa, Palomino, Paint and Pinto, Albino, and Buckskin registries, to name a few — and a horse of the wrong color or pattern may not be registered with them, although it may have the desired conformation. Other registries may permit only particular colors or patterns. Pinto patterns are barred from the majority of breed registries, for instance.

Since names for horse colors do not compare with nonhorse color names, a definition of each color becomes a necessity.

Black: all the hair is completely black without any brown hairs.

Brown: a brown horse may look black. The only way to determine which it is, is to examine the areas around the eyes and muzzle for lighter hairs.

Bay: a bay horse is some shade of red or auburn with black mane, tail, and stockings. A very dark bay, mahogany bay, is much like a brown horse. A bay with a red coat is a blood bay, and a bay with a tan coat is a sandy bay. The sandy bay resembles a buckskin, except that it has no dorsal stripe and is somewhat redder.

Chestnut: a chestnut has the same range of colors as the bay, but its mane, tail, and stockings are the same color or lighter than the coat color. Further description is given in the Suffolk Punch section.

Gray: a gray horse is born black or brown and lightens with age, becomes nearly white as it matures. The Lipizzan is a gray horse.

Roan: a roan coat has an even sprinkling of white and sometimes red and yellow hairs among the hairs of the base color of the coat. White hairs in a black coat produce a blue roan. A roaned bay is called a red roan, and a roaned chestnut is called a strawberry roan.

Palomino: the Palomino is gold or yellow with white mane and tail. A full description of the Palomino may be found in that section.

Dun or Buckskin: a yellow coat with black mane, tail, and stockings, and an eel stripe or dorsal stripe down the back. There are sometimes stripes (barring) on the legs and shoulders. For a more complete discussion, see the Buckskin section.

Cream: sometimes called cremello, a cream-colored horse is pale yellow with either white or yellow mane and tail. The Cream Draft Horse is this color.

White or Albino: a true white horse (not a faded gray) is born white or very nearly so. The American Albino is the best example of white coloring, and more information will be found in that section.

Pinto and Appaloosa patterns are discussed in the Pinto and Appaloosa sections.

White markings on the face and legs are found with every coat color. They have no connection with pinto markings unless they are extensive, stretching up above the knee and hock or over the sides of the face.

Most horses have three gaits or way of moving: the walk, the trot, and the canter (the canter is a slow gallop; the gallop is also called the run).

All horses walk — the Mustang and the Icelandic Pony, shown on pages 59 and 121 are walking. Nearly all horses trot — the Morgan and the Hackney Pony shown on pages 55 and 117 are trotting. The trot of the pony is a collected trot (collected means performing with good action and poise but going forward slowly. When the Lipizzan performs the *piaffe*, it trots without moving forward at all). Horses that do not trot, either through training or breeding, may pace, as the Standardbred on page 83 is doing, or *paso* as the Peruvian Paso and the Paso Fino are doing on pages 67 and 63. Or they may perform the fox-trot, the rack, or the running walk, as the Tennessee Walking Horse on page 87 is doing. The gallop is the fastest gait of the horse. The Thoroughbred on page 91 is galloping. Other movements may be taught the horse, such as the *capriole* being done by the Lipizzan, page 47. Discussions of the various gaits may be found in the sections on the American Saddle Horse, Paso Fino, Peruvian Paso, Missouri Fox Trotter, and the Tennessee Walking Horse.

Man has brought the horse a long way in the trek from scrubby little wild pony to modern pleasure horse. But he seldom stops to think of what the horse was before man domesticated him — what the horse was before man knew him — what the horse was before man had even climbed down out of his tree.

COLOR BREEDS

Albino

Outstanding points of conformation:

_____

HEIGHT: from minimum pony height to maximum draft and light horse height.
COLORS AND MARKINGS: pure white body coat, mane, and tail, with no darker hairs anywhere.
EYES: brown or dark blue. Light blue and white eyes not allowed.

AN AMERICAN ALBINO HORSE breeder is a peculiar sort of person who is likely to spend (and greatly enjoy) inordinate lengths of time poring over genetics books and his horses' bloodlines. For, successfully producing American Albino Horses is a science, and if the breeder is to have any good results at all he must do his homework diligently.

He is trying to get a Dominant White foal, a snow-white foal with pink skin, brown or dark blue eyes (never white), and no darker spots or hairs anywhere in the body coat, mane, or tail. If he has planned carefully and bred the proper stallion to the proper mare, there is still a 5 percent chance that the foal will be some other color, such as ivory, cream, palomino, or even some dark color like bay or roan. Its eyes may be white or very light blue, or it may have a beautiful white body coat and dark eyes, but a sooty mane and tail.

The reason for the 5 percent chance of failure is that the white coat and dark eyes combination (called Dominant White by the American Albino Horse Club, AAHC) is not actually a real albino.

A real albino would have pink eyes and would probably breed true each time. The Dominant White does not breed true each time because with each mating some off-color genes may be transmitted and carried on in the bloodlines, even if the offspring is Dominant White. Palomino breeders have the same problem with color.

Chances of predicting a Dominant White foal are much higher than they once were, for the AAHC has taken a farsighted stand and registers under a separate "Classification" section all ivory- and cream-colored horses, and even the dark-colored horses (or off-white), as they are celled by the AAHC), which have produced Dominant White foals in an effort to clarify the genetics situation. Thus far, they have found thirteen different types of white horses, each one of which gives different breeding results. The AAHC records are surprisingly complete, and include eye and coat color of each off-white horse used and the eye and coat color of its parents and grandparents, if known.

The American Albino Horse Club is an open registry, allowing outside blood to be registered, but it nevertheless has its individual strains and bloodlines extending back to Old King, a small white horse standing only 15:2 hands, who was born in 1906 of possibly Arabian-Morgan blood. He was sturdy, with a short, strong back, and had a well-rounded barrel and good legs. Bred almost exclusively to colored Morgan mares, his get was predominantly white. These offspring were the foundation stock of most registered Albinos of today.

In 1937, the AAHC was formed on the White Horse Ranch near Naper, Nebraska, for purposes of promoting the various types of albinos that were being produced on the ranch. At that time, the ranch could satisfy people who wanted white ponies, draft horses, western horses, gaited and walking horses. Since then the ranchers have conducted extensive breeding programs with American Saddle Horse, Standardbred, and Thoroughbred infusions. Horses registered within other breeds may become registered Albinos if they meet the requirements. Many other breed registries will not allow Albino horses within their ranks. In some registries, a Palomino will be entered in the books whereas an Albino with exactly the same breeding will be barred. In most breeds, however, white coloring is frowned upon because it indicates outside breeding if no white coloration had appeared before the registry was closed to outside blood.

Ponies are registered separately from horses, the ponies being 14:2 hands and under. The breeding of most of the smaller ponies is Welsh and Shetland, but the remainder are a pot-pourri of various breeds. They should have the conformation of whatever type they fall into.

Albino horses and ponies are bred for good conformation and disposition, spirit, action, gentleness, and intelligence. These attributes are necessary if the albino is to please its owner and admirers.

White horses are frequently used in exhibitions, circuses, fairs, advertising, and movie productions, for there is something about a white horse that catches the imagination. The Lone Ranger would not have been quite as great without his wonderful horse Silver, and comic books about the adventures of Silver and his wild herd have had high sales. In old westerns, one can spot the "good guy" right away, because he's riding the white horse. It goes back a very long way — a knight in armor would have seemed less pure and potent had he been mounted on anything but a snow-white charger (that same knight — or one a lot like him — has advertised detergent on television for ages). Lady Godiva rode a white horse, too.

The American Albino will probably be around for quite a while. Now that extensive breeding records are available to breeders, some sires can boast 100 percent white foals when bred to white mares. The breed seems to be stabilizing, and hopefully, perhaps someday it will be possible to get Dominant White foals every time.

Buckskin

Outstanding points of conformation:

HEIGHT: from minimum pony height to maximum light horse height.
COLORS AND MARKINGS: buckskin with black points (eel stripe and barring desirable but not required), red dun with dark red points (eel stripe required), and grulla (eel stripe required). White markings are frowned upon and are permitted only below the knee and hock, and on the face. Barring resembles zebra striping and is often found on the legs.

THE OLD COWPOKE of the early West had nothing but admiration for the buckskin pony. From his well-filled reservoir of horse information he would, without much urging, present item after item about the dun's tremendous endurance, its stamina and weight-carrying ability, its tough feet that could trot a rocky trail for long distances without shoes and with little sign of wear, and its strong legs that never seemed to tire. Perhaps he exaggerated sometimes, but the basis for his information was solid, and he would choose a dun above most other colors any time.

The buckskin wasn't invariably called a dun. If it were some shade of yellow or gold with black points and maybe an eel stripe and barring on the legs, it was called a buckskin. If it were pinkish or reddish, with dark red legs, mane, and tail, it was a red dun or claybank. The oddest dun, though, was the grullo or grulla (pronounced groo-ay and meaning "crane" in Spanish, presumably because its color was like that of the blue crane's). It was a bluish or lavender color with black points and an eel stripe. Sometimes the color bordered on salt-and-pepper, for the slate color was due to an even sprinkling of white hairs all over the body. It was also called mouse dun and coyote dun. These colors all may be found among horses today, and the American Buckskin Registry Association, formed in 1962, registers them all, provided they have good conformation, are not of draft horse ancestry, and have no indication of pinto or Appaloosa breeding.

It is commendable that someone besides the cowboy has come along to champion the buckskin and his dun brothers. The buckskin has been too much relegated to back corners and accidental appearances in other breeds, for it has a lot of merit in its own right as an individual color and type.

The lineage of the buckskin goes back a long way, but in a broken line. Most buckskins in America are descended from Spanish Barbs through the mustangs and Quarter Horses, from northern European ponies imported for children, and from breeds in America with old Norfolk Trotter bloodlines, for the Norfolk Trotter was descended from the Norwegian Dun, which in turn was directly descended from the Tarpan, a very strong grulla. The Arabian horse has never had dun colors in its assortment, and this is part of the reason that in many breeds dun is either excluded or discouraged, breeders apparently feeling that it, like pinto markings, denotes lowly breeding. This unfortunate policy has excluded some of the most striking animals from becoming a more common sight. Where there is a strong concentration of buckskin blood, the coat is bright and the black points and eel stripes are outstanding. In addition, a pure buckskin may have a shoulder stripe, varying from just a shadow to a very wide dark mark. And on its legs there often appear stripes very much like a zebra's. Where buckskin blood is quite concentrated, faint stripes may be seen over the entire body. They are in the same configuration as zebra stripes, but much narrower and usually not very dark.

The stripes are quite welcome among buckskin breeders, and even sought after. The American Buckskin Registry Association (ABRA) uses sound principles in selecting buckskins for registry, which puts it one notch above the ordinary color registry. Requirements state that in order to be considered, the horse (or pony) must have the proper coloring, but any animal of correct coloring will be rejected if it has below-average conformation. Color is not considered in judging animals at horse shows, for this would tend to put color above conformation, leading to an ultimate deterioration in conformation. Horses may be registered in other associations, also, being Quarter Horses, for instance (as most are), or any other light horse or pony breed.

Some of the requirements are that the skin be black, that there be no white spots on the body (even white leg markings below the knees are frowned upon, but allowed under the assumption that they will breed out in offspring if the blood strength is increased in future matings; white face markings are also permitted), and that the red dun and grulla must have the dorsal stripe, although it isn't required in the buckskin. A dun is born almost creamy white, and only turns color when the baby hair sheds out.

Grulla is one of the more scarce colors registered in ABRA.

To get it, some breeders cross buckskin on gray. The gulla thus obtained isn't a pure grulla, but it is registered if it has a dorsal stripe. All too often, the progeny of this matching turns ordinary gray by maturity.

The registry is still open, and should be for several years more to draw a good nucleus of stock. It is good to see a place being made for this ancient color among the other breeds and colors.

Palomino

Outstanding points of conformation:

HEIGHT: 14 to 17 hands.
COLORS AND MARKINGS: since this is a color breed, the only color allowed is gold with white mane and tail, white markings permitted.
GENERAL CONFORMATION: any conformation which is acceptable as proper conformation for a light horse breed.
MANE AND TAIL: always white, left long except where the animal is used in western classes, in which case they're trimmed western fashion.

THE PALOMINO is, without any doubt or argument, a color breed. Nearly all the requirements qualifying a palomino for registration with the Palomino Horse Breeders of America (PHBA) have to do with color, although there are a few general rules about conformation and type. For instance, the horse must not be of draft breeding, and must stand between 14 and 17 hands. It must have conformation and refinement appropriate to its other breed. Only the elite horse is eligible, for either its sire or dam must be listed with the PHBA or with the Remount, Arabian, Quarter-Horse, American Saddle Horse, Jockey Club, Morgan, Palomino Horse Association, Tennessee Walking Horse, or Standardbred registries. The only exceptions are geldings, who can be registered if they meet color and conformation standards, regardless of parentage. The Palomino Horse Association has much the same color and conformation standards, but it is not as restrictive regarding pedigree.

Breeding for palomino coloring is a chancy business. There is never any guarantee that the breeder will get a palomino since the color is not "fixed," that is, the genetics pose problems that prevent palomino to palomino crosses from consistently producing palomino foals. In such crosses, about half the get will be albinos and chestnuts, the other half will be palominos. A more certain cross is to breed a palomino with a sorrel, for the sorrel genes prevent at least the occurrence of white skin and light eyes and hooves in the offspring. The PHBA bars palominos with one albino parent, and this is most unfortunate, for there is virtually a 100 percent certainty of producing palomino foals only when the right sort of albino is bred to a chestnut. As with the albino-chestnut cross, there are many unlikely crosses that will occasionally produce the genetically unstable palomino. For instance: dun-brown, sorrel-gray, dun-roan, sorrel-dun, sorrel-sorrel, dun-dun, and several other crosses. The PHBA takes great pains to avoid pinto breeding, designating that no registered palomino shall have white markings other than on the face and below the knees (except that a thin line of white might run up six inches above the hock on the rear legs). Glass eyes are barred, as are blue or pink eyes, although they may be black, brown, or hazel. The skin must be black or at least dark except where it is under a white marking; and the color of the coat is strictly regulated, any zebra striping or dorsal stripe being banned, as are darker or lighter patches of hair. The mane and tail are to be white without more than 15 percent dark hair mixed in (this ruling is always open to debate since it is difficult to determine how much 15 percent is when dealing with mixed hair). The required color of the golden coat is also open to discussion, for the PHBA ambiguously states that the palomino horse must be the color of a newly minted United States gold coin, and it is highly unlikely that very many palomino breeders, judges, or admirers have ever seen a United States gold coin, since the government ceased to mint them several decades ago.

There is another kind of palomino, and although the PHBA does not register it, the PHA does. The difference between the two is that the second kind has a pink or yellow skin instead of black. The coat of the light-skinned palomino stays gold the year around, with the winter coat slightly darker, but the dark-skinned palomino's coat may turn cream or white in the winter, only regaining its golden sheen when the winter coat sheds out.

Most palominos are also registered Quarter Horses, and they average somewhere around 50 percent of the total number of registered palominos. The second most numerous breed in the palomino registries is the American Saddle Horse, and the other breeds have palomino members in diminishing numbers. Whatever the breed, the palomino is always viewed with a great deal of pleasure and pride, for everyone turns to look at a palomino, whether it be working cattle or leading a parade. The light horse doesn't have a corner on the golden color, however, for palomino coloration appears in ponies and draft horses on occasion. It seems to have been most prevalent in horses of Spanish extraction, and when Queen Isabella reigned in Spain long ages ago, she mounted her troops on palominos named Ysabellas in her honor.

Perhaps the charm of the palomino lies not only in its color but also in its fickleness. For to create a palomino requires skill in selecting promising parents as well as a great deal of luck in the outcome, and it will probably always be that way, much to the palomino admirer's sorrow.

Prehistoric Horses

THE STORY OF prehistoric horse is one of the most fascinating and best documented histories of any prehistoric animal, for there are fossils from nearly every phase of its long existence, beginning about sixty million years ago in a time known as the Eocene (see chart).

This first horse didn't look like a horse, or act like a horse, and certainly hadn't descended from anything even vaguely resembling a horse. But a horse it was, and in sixty million years it was to become the companion and servant of man all over the world. The story is not a very complicated one, but in order to understand it well, it is necessary first to have a grasp of how evolution works.

The word evolution involves several ideas. In general, it means that over long periods of time, living things change in form, intelligence, and distribution over the world, in such a way that every living thing is suited to take fullest advantage of the conditions surrounding it. These changes take place not from year to year but from century to century (what man does in the way of changing plants and animals over a short space of time is not called evolution) so that they are scarcely noticeable from one thousand-year period to the next.

A horse can't change itself or its young in order to adapt to new conditions — it has no control over what its young will be like. But if a horse has a foal which is slightly different in a way that makes it faster, smarter, or better able to compete with other animals, that one foal will be more likely to survive and produce offspring like itself. Changes (mutations) may occur often or seldom in the history of a race, but those mutated animals best suited

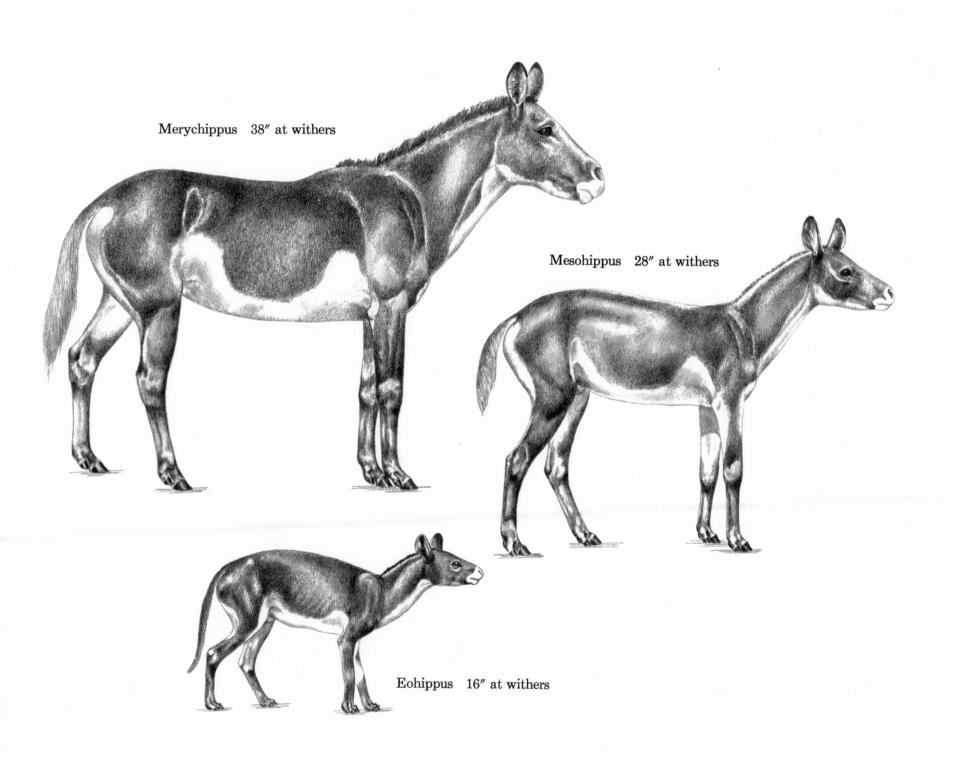

Merychippus   38″ at withers

Mesohippus   28″ at withers

Eohippus   16″ at withers

to the environment will succeed and eventually replace the others. On the other hand, if no beneficial changes happen while the environment is changing, the animals will not be able to cope with the new conditions and will die out. Both these things have happened in the long history of the horse.

From a strange little animal called the Condylarth (con-di-larth) evolved many of the hoofed animals on earth today, including the horse. The horse is most closely related to the tapir of South America and the rhinoceros of Africa and Asia. Many of the Condylarths had hooves, but some had claws instead. One type of Condylarth, a creature called Phenacodus (fen-ack-o-duss) was the immediate ancestor of the horse. It was probably omnivorous (eating both meat and plants) and it looked like a cross between an aardvark and a dog. A rangy animal, its head was small and its tail was long and ropelike. Its feet were padded, much like a dog's; each foot had five toes, each toe had its own little hoof. There is a short gap in our information between Phenacodus and the first real horse, eohippus (ee-o-hip-pus), but there is no doubt that Phenacodus fathered the horse in the early Eocene.

By minute and nearly indistinguishable changes, there finally emerged from the doggish Phenacodus a primitive little herbivore suited to browsing on soft leaves and shrubbery. It came in various sizes from ten to twenty inches tall. It had an arched and flexible back, a long tail, and a high, rabbity croup. The lower bones of its legs were fairly short, and on the front legs were four toes each, while the back feet had three toes, each toe ending in a little hoof. It carried most of its weight on its middle toe, and on a pad between the toes almost like a dog does today. Its head was long and thin with the eyes halfway between the nose and the back of the head, and the nose was neatly tapered. The teeth were

| RECENT: began 25,000 years ago. |
| EQUUS spread over world only last 400 years. |
| MAN's agriculture began 7,000 years ago. |

| PLEISTOCENE: began 1 million years ago. |
| EQUUS |
| PRIMITIVE MAN, had fire, but no agriculture. |
| Forests and plains striking balance, major glaciations. |
| Climate similar to that of today. |

| PLIOCENE: began 10 million years ago. |
| PLIOHIPPUS |
| ADVANCED MANLIKE APES |
| Climate cooling and drying, plains widespread. |

| MIOCENE: began 25 million years ago. |
| MERYCHIPPUS |
| PARAHIPPUS |
| MANLIKE APES |
| Land becoming open, plains prevalent with grasses evolving and spreading to cover them; increased rates of earth movements (earthquakes, volcanic action, etc.) and erosion with major mountain ranges forming. |

| OLIGOCENE: began 35 million years ago. |
| MIOHIPPUS |
| MESOHIPPUS |
| Land less wooded, plains increasing in size, climate ranging from subtropical to temperate, little change caused by earth movements. |

| EOCENE: began 55 million years ago. |
| EPIHIPPUS |
| OROHIPPUS |
| EOHIPPUS |
| Land mostly wooded, climate cooling to subtropical temperatures, topsoil forming more rapidly from increased earth movements and erosion. |

| PALEOCENE: began 70 million years ago. |
| CONDYLARTH |
| Land mostly wooded, climate semitropical, land not being much changed by erosion or earth movements. |

small and rounded, somewhat like a modern human's, and its brain looked much like a reptile's. This was the first horse, eohippus or Hyracotherium (hi-rack-o-ther-ium), and it was so extremely numerous that it roamed both North America and Europe and left abundant fossils in both. Hyracotherium was first discovered and named in England in 1838. Its identity as a horse wasn't even suspected at the time, and it was given the scientific name Hyracotherium which means "hyrax-like beast" (a hyrax is a rodent which looks something like a guinea pig). Fossils later found in America were given the name Eohippus, meaning "dawn horse," which is scientifically a much more correct name. When it was discovered that it was the same animal as Hyracotherium, the original name had to be proclaimed as the proper one since it was given first. This is why both terms exist today, and it is proper to use eohippus only in uncapitalized form as a common name, the same as "horse" or "cow."

Eohippus lived at a time when grass had barely begun to develop, so it had a choice of soft plants and shrub leaves as a diet. It probably lived along watercourses and in swamps where vegetation was fairly soft; for its teeth were small and fragile, fit only for chewing soft plants during a short life span. Eohippus was probably a stupid animal, having a tiny, primitive brain, but its fleetness and great numbers insured it a degree of safety.

By tiny changes, eohippus evolved into a slightly different animal called Orohippus (or-o-hip-pus). It was no larger than the original, but its teeth were better constructed for chewing tougher vegetation. This gave it an edge, for it had a larger variety of things to eat. Orohippus and its descendant Epihippus (ep-ih-hip-pus), which was the same size but with still more efficient teeth, lived until the end of the Eocene, thirty-five million years ago.

The land was changing during this time. It was transforming from swamps into a rivers-and-plains environment, and grass was becoming plentiful — an excellent food supply for horses if they could only eat it. But as yet they were not grazers but browsers only, and would be for millions of years to come.

Orohippus presented very little outward change from eohippus, but Epihippus gradually began to lose the fourth outside toe on the front foot, and its decendant Mesohippus (mess-o-hip-pus), which appeared in the Oligocene, was the first horse to have three toes front and back. Some members of Mesohippus were no larger than eohippus, but most averaged twenty-four inches tall or 6 hands, while a few overshot this height by several inches. Mesohippus had a long and slender body, a neck that tended to be heavier and shorter than its ancestors' necks were, and a back with still quite a bit of flexibility and arch. Its head had become more horsey in appearance, although the face was narrow and the jaws shallow. The eyes were more toward the rear of the head than they had been in earlier horses. Its legs were slender, longer from knee to hock, and a pad was still present between the toes. On the front foot, the fourth toe remained as a little knob at the fetlock. The toes were more closely grouped and the legs were losing their flexibility, being confined mostly to back-and-forth movement. Mesohippus had a much larger and more complex brain than had eohippus, which is probably why it had prospered.

Mesohippus graduated so evenly and quietly into an animal called Miohippus (my-o-hip-pus) that scientists argue about where the dividing line should be. The teeth of Miohippus were improved and its back ankles were stronger and wider, but it was still a browser, ignoring grass. Its importance lies in the fact that with Miohippus the horse story became complicated, for it spread into several branches, some of which flourished for a long time.

Miohippus lived twenty-five million years ago in the early Miocene when the environment was rich and varied. There was a choice of different environments, such as deep forest, swamp, and open plain and savanna, with abundant new plants appearing and spreading. From Miohippus came large, medium-sized, and even dwarfed horses, all with different structures and tooth designs suited to various environments. Some had a traveling urge that took them far into Eurasia. The branch of Miohippus in which we take the most interest, however, is Parahippus (pair-uh-hip-pus) from which evolved Merychippus (mair-ee-kip-pus) which had finally developed grazing teeth.

We know that grass was widespread and plentiful in the Miocene because numerous fossil grass seeds are found in deposits of clay laid down during that epoch. Merychippus, a long-bodied horse standing about 10 hands, had good grinding teeth. They were long and strong enough to chew tough grasses over a long life span. As a consequence of having such long teeth, its jaw was much deeper and its skull looked more like a modern horse's skull. Its eyes were nearly as far toward the rear as they are in a modern horse, and in all, it resembled today's horse rather closely except that each foot still had three toes and hooves. The outside toes were becoming smaller, and the whole foot looked like a modern pig's foot except for having one central toe instead of two.

The little hooves on the sides were probably useful for two purposes in Merychippus and its forerunners. Surely little eohippus had found them extremely useful for getting around in the swamps (to use the pig as an example: the wild pig is a forest animal and finds its side hooves necessary for supporting it on soft ground). In addition, the side toes were useful for taking up part of the shock each time the foot hit the ground, for Merychippus and its progenitors hadn't yet developed the tough, springlike, shock-absorbing tendon that the modern horse has between hock and toe. Early horse may have had to depend upon the side toes to take up shock which otherwise would have stretched and strained foot muscles. With Merychippus the side toes were diminishing in size. The fact that Merychippus was successful in spite of the size reduction indicates that the toes were becoming less necessary for survival. Since Merychippus was a plains dweller, it would seldom need the side toes for use on marshy earth. And the structure of its leg and foot bones indicate that the ligaments later so well developed in modern horse were becoming larger and therefore stronger, making the side toes unnecessary for efficient locomotion.

Although diminishing side toes seemed to be the coming thing, Hipparion (hip-air-ee-un), a branch of horses which evolved from Merychippus, retained three toes on each hoof, and its descendant Stylohipparion (sty-lo-hip-air-ee-un) survived for about twenty million years — existing alongside primitive zebras during the Pleistocene in Africa.

Besides Hipparion, Merychippus gave rise to several other ultimately unsuccessful branches of horses. The only one to survive the Pleistocene was Pliohippus (ply-o-hip-pus), which originated in the late Miocene, fifteen million years ago. It was the only horse of them all to lose its side toes. Remains of the toes were still found to be found under the skin (even as they are today in the form of splint bones), but it truly had only one hoof on each foot. This toe disappearance was no sudden thing, for the toes had gradually gotten smaller over several million years. The teeth of Pliohippus were longer than those of any previous horse, and the jaws were deeper to accommodate them. For some reason not yet determined, there was a deep pocket or hollow in front of each eye socket. In general shape and size, Pliohippus was like a modern pony. By the end of the Pliocene, Pliohippus had changed to such an extent that it received a new name: *Equus*.

Questions about the color and coat pattern of prehistoric horse continually arise. There is no way to know, of course, for fossils give no indication of color. A look at some of the northern ponies suggests that early horses of Europe and Asia were zebra-striped. Donkeys and northern ponies are often heavily striped on the legs and sometimes even over the shoulders and flanks, with a pattern of fine zebra markings on the face. The stripes of the zebra provide an excellent reason for suspecting stripes on early horses, for the modern zebra is a relatively primitive horse. A zebra without its stripes looks much like a horse. The Quagga is considered to have been well on its way to solid coloring, for it was missing nearly half its stripes by the time it was exterminated. Early horse, then, might easily have been striped.

Little eohippus would have been well camouflaged in the forest had it been spotted like a deer. Today spots are quite frequently found among modern horses as well as the more primitive Mongolian and Chinese ponies. The Appaloosa provides excellent examples of the spot patterns which may be found. These spots may be a repeat of an extremely ancient pattern or they may be merely a recent variation.

Given such a wide choice of spots and stripes, we can assign early horses almost any variety of markings imaginable, from zebra stripes and Appaloosa spots to the stripe-spot pattern of the immature tapir.

The wanderings of prehistoric horse were truly epic. Eohippus was originally found in both America and Europe. But the European eohippus and the American eohippus were separated for several million years by the disappearance of the land bridge across what are now the Bering Straits. This bridge connected Alaska and Siberia during the early Eocene. While the American eohippus changed and prospered, its European counterpart also changed, but died out near the end of the Eocene.

Although the land bridge was again in existence in the early and middle Oligocene (during the time that Mesohippus and Miohippus were developing) no migrations took place, and for a time there were no horse-type animals on the Eurasian continent. This land bridge would sink and rise again before any horses would cross it.

As the eons rolled by and the descendants of eohippus developed into more complex animals, side branches of the horse family migrated again and again into Asia and Europe. But it wasn't until the late Pliocene that any horse invaded South America. Until that time it had been separated from the North American continent by water. The horse to make the southward trek was Pliohippus, the direct ancestor of *Equus*. However, its descendants were apparently substandard, for they were ousted by later migrations of *Equus* in almost the form we know it today.

Forerunners of the modern horse entered Eurasia in the late Pliocene and Pleistocene in the form of *Equus*. As a result of their appearance in Eurasia, they eventually replaced all earlier forms of the horse; and with that migration, which lasted about a million years and ended only ten thousand years ago, the horse suddenly became extinct in both North and South America. The reason has yet to be found for such a swift disappearance. The current guesses are that they were beset by some virulent disease, or that the Indians (who were beginning to settle North and South America by this time) assisted in their extinction. It has come to light that similar disappearances of large animals have occurred on various continents and islands with the appearance of early man. It is possible that early man in his efforts to obtain the meat of one or two animals exterminated large herds by means of fire or by chasing them over cliffs. It is known that plains Indians of America drove great herds of buffalo over precipices to get meat and hides although they couldn't utilize all the meat and hides thus made available and much was wasted. It has been hypothesized that such animals as the deer and buffalo of Pleistocene times survived because they retreated from the open plains to the woods and mountains where they couldn't be slaughtered en masse.

There are no fossil clues of any large predator (besides man) having come suddenly on the scene to decimate the horse's ranks to such low numbers that it could not survive. This disappearance is one of the unsolved mysteries for which we may never have the provable answer.

Equus settled in various places in Europe, Asia, and Africa. Those members who traveled the farthest were the progenitors of the Mountain Zebra and the Common Zebra, for they migrated to the tip of Africa. Grévy's Zebra ended up on the eastern edge of central Africa along with the wild asses. The Onager settled in the south and central parts of Asia. The Tarpan and Przewalski's Horse, both of the species *Equus caballus,* from which come the horses of today, settled in Europe, Russia, and central Asia, their ranges overlapping in places.

Of the two, the Tarpan has finer features and what horsemen call style; and although there is no proof, there are some who claim that the Tarpan was the forerunner of the Arabian Horse, while Przewalski's Horse fathered all ponies and heavy breeds of Europe. Fossil remains found in Europe indicate that there may have been a large, ancestral horse in the low, marshy parts of Europe which produced the forerunners of the draft horse.

Some horse owners insist that their fine show horses could not possibly have come from such coarse stock as Przewalski's Horse, or even from the Tarpan, and that surely there must have been some other superior type *Equus* available to the first horse tamers. There is no proof for this, and really no need for such a claim, for several thousand years of domestication have greatly altered the shape of man's beast of burden.

Man himself has instituted most of the changes in the horse. For instance, by choosing certain desirable features in one horse and mating it to a horse with similar features (this seldom happens in nature), and by carefully controlling the breeding of the offspring, a strain of horses can be radically transformed in the course of a few generations. It can be made large, small, slim, heavy — or with special features such as a fine, long mane and tail or yellow eyes — to cite only a few characters that can be selected through controlled breeding. Some form of controlled selection has probably been practiced ever since man began breeding his own horses.

Whatever differences existed between and among the ancestors of the various types of horses and ponies, they fade into insignificance when compared to the changes man has made in a few short centuries. It might be said that a hundred years of inbreeding by man is worth a million years of evolution.

The person who gets involved in trying to trace origins of the various European breeds of horses and their various movements over Asia, the Mediterranean, and Europe finds himself wading through pages and pages of contradictory literature. Most of the confusion stems from arguments over the origin of the Arabian Horse, where it came from, and where it went in the Old World.

We don't know exactly when man began to domesticate the horse. It was most certainly many thousands of years after he had begun eating him, for it is known from ancient bone heaps that Stone Age man ate horsemeat regularly. Historical records were not being made during the first hundreds of years in the saga of horse and man. The earliest records of domesticated horses appear in about 2000 B.C. in both China and Mesopotamia. Since travel between these opposite ends of Asia was probably unheard of, it seems likely that horse domestication began almost simultaneously in both areas. In other areas, such as Europe and Russia, which were not yet keeping written records, it is likely that horse taming was proceeding at a comparable rate. If this is true, the "original domesticated breed" of Asia was not one strain but many, all capable of interbreeding.

Arabia and surrounding areas aren't and weren't at that time especially hospitable places for horse raising. Forage and water were scant and not of the best quality, and the horse probably would not have chosen the Arabian deserts as its range without the insistence of man. There are several theories about the origins of the Arabian Horse, but no written records offer proof for any of them.

Three thousand years ago, domesticated horses could be found in all parts of Asia, North Africa, and Europe, and they most certainly weren't all of the "hot-blooded" or Arabian type. Except for Europe's large heavy breeds, most horses were pony size, as depicted on Roman and Grecian sculptures and friezes, and most were used for war purposes.

Wars have accounted for nearly all the recent spread of horses throughout the world, aside from their original migrations. The conquest of the Mongolians (Attila the Hun and company) and the conquering surge of Arabian Mohammedans spread Asian horses throughout all parts of the Near East, North Africa, and southern Europe. The only thing capable of stopping the march of the Arabs and their lithe ponies were the impregnable heavy war-horses and their mail-clad riders in France. Whatever the effects of the war itself, the results of the introduction of small swift desert horses (hot blood) into the realm of the massive charger (cold blood) were profound.

Thus began the matching of hot and cold blood to produce the riding horse, the draft horse, and the utility horse of Europe. Periodic invasion and peacetime trading introduced fresh stock from time to time. In Spain, a mixture of this sort consisting of Barb, Arabian, and coarse native blood produced a useful little horse called the Spanish Jennet or Jineta. It was the jennet that was transported across the Atlantic Ocean to the New World (again in the interests of war — this time against the Aztecs) and which became the mustang of the Americas.

Those who are seriously interested in detailed accounts of horse movements in Europe, Asia, and Africa throughout the ages can find plenty of material for their study. They would do well, however, to read several different sources before deciding what to believe about the widely divergent theories.

Light Horses

LIGHT HORSES HAVE some common points of conformation, whether they be saddle horses bred for pleasure riding, stock horses designed for utility work, or light harness horses used for pulling featherweight conveyances in the show ring. All should have some points in common, although each breed signals its differences from the others by especially good, large, or small development of one or several points of its makeup.

In the following list are given the average light horse's ideal points of conformation. Few breeds or breed members possess all of these points, and if all horses had all of them all there would be no distinctive breeds. So when considering conformation in each breed, it would be well to keep in mind the extra and different ideals that any given breed might be aiming for.

To properly evaluate the conformation of a horse, it should be shown standing squarely on all legs, for if the animal is posed in a stretched position, it is possible to overlook many conformation defects — it is likely that this is the reason that many horse-show exhibitors prefer the stretched stance for their horses.

Outstanding points of conformation:

HEIGHT: between 14:2 and 16:3 hands. A hand is equal to four inches, the width of an average man's hand. Animals shorter than this are ponies, and those taller are usually not good riding animals.

HEAD: should show characteristics common to the breed of horse it represents. It should be possible to tell the breeding of the horse by looking at the head.

EARS: should be attached well and show alertness; should not be especially large or small unless this is a breed trait.

EYES: the ideal eye is bright, large, alert, and set well to the sides of the head in a prominent position.

FOREHEAD: there should be much width between the eyes.

PROFILE: this is extremely variable among breeds.

MUZZLE AND NOSTRILS: should present a boxlike appearance, with the nostrils large and high on a square muzzle, with firm lips.

JAW: there should be considerable depth through the jaw when viewed from the side.

NECK: should join with the head at a wide angle and should be moderately long and smooth. A very cresty neck should be avoided. The neck should blend into the shoulder and chest smoothly.

MANE: should be shiny and healthy looking.

SHOULDERS: ideally set at a forty-five-degree angle for the smoothest ride; a straight shoulder gives a jolting ride. Muscling on the shoulder should be flat and smooth.

CHEST: should be wide and deep but not particularly bulging.

WITHERS: must be prominent, not flat, not knifelike, for the proper fitting of the saddle. It is almost impossible to keep a saddle properly positioned on a flat-withered horse, especially if it is an active animal like a hunter or jumper.

FOREARM: muscles should be long and abundant, for these are the only lifting muscles in the entire leg.

KNEES: should be broad and flat, with a large joint.

CANNONS, FORE AND REAR: should be very short and have much width from front to back, but narrow when viewed from the front.

FETLOCKS, FORE AND REAR: should be large, square joints.

PASTERNS, FORE AND REAR: medium length and slope are desirable. Too long a pastern is poor since it will weaken and strain, but too short a pastern gives a jolting ride and the shock of each step will crunch joints in knee and shoulder together, causing unsoundness.

HOOVES, FORE AND REAR: must be large in circumference, deep and long at the heel, and widely open at the back.

UNDERLINE: is the profile of the belly from the point just behind the elbows to where it is met by the stifle. It should be moderately full and not drawn up at the rear, for a drawn-up belly indicates a restriction in the capacity of the vital organs and a consequent inability of the horse to make the best use of its food.

RIBS: should be well sprung and rounded; the horse should not be flat-sided.

BACK: is the area from just behind the withers to the loin or coupling. It should be short with heavy muscling.

LOIN OR COUPLING: heavy muscling is required in order that the horse may bear weight on its back without strain.

CROUP: the leveler it is, the better; it should be well muscled, broad, and as long as possible.

TAIL: should be attached well up on the croup, not drooping, and the hair should be healthy looking.

HIP: the hip also should be strong and well muscled, for this is where the horse gets its propelling power.

THIGH: the muscling in the hip should carry down evenly into the thigh and to the stifle. At the stifle, when viewed from the rear of the horse, more width will be apparent than at any other point on its body.

GASKIN: the gaskin must also be heavily muscled, and somewhat bulging, for this helps drive the leg.

HOCK: should be a large joint, proportional to the rest of the horse, wide, smooth, and flat.

21

American Saddle Horse

Outstanding points of conformation:

HEIGHT: 15 to 16 hands.
COLORS AND MARKINGS: chestnut, bay, black, and brown most common; white markings often seen.
EARS: small and slender.
FACE: flat.
NECK: gracefully arched, longer than any other breed.
FEET: medium size, but grown very long for showing.
BACK: extremely short.
CROUP: well below wither height.
MANE AND TAIL: hair is fine and as thick as possible. On five-gaited horses, tail and mane are left full and long, the tail being set. On three-gaited horses, tail is shaved or pulled for the first nine inches, the rest being left full, and the mane is roached. The tail of the three-gaited horse is also set.

THE AMERICAN SADDLE HORSE is one of the most beautiful and at the same time often the most unfortunate horse in the world. Its long, graceful neck and airy animated carriage give it the look of an aristocrat, and its brilliant action sometimes rivals that of the Hackney. Some are bred primarily for use as show horses, and it is these horses which might well be called unfortunate. Many, for instance, are so pampered that they have never tasted green grass. From birth to retirement they are never turned out to pasture for fear that they will get scratched or pull out mane or tail hair in a fence or tree. What a dull life for a spirited horse!

The American Saddle Horse wasn't always a show horse. Its beginnings are ancient, stretching back to colonial times nearly four hundred years ago. It was a combination of English riding horse with English Barb and Arabian breeding, brought to America by the original settlers. More Arabian and Barb blood was added, using oriental stock imported to the Colonies. The forerunner of the American Saddle Horse was the Kentucky Saddle Horse, an established breed as long ago as 1830, and to this strain was added the blood of the Standardbred, Morgan, and a preponderance of Thoroughbred. The official foundation sire was Denmark, a race horse of Thoroughbred and Arabian blood. The breed became established more or less as it is today with the formation of the American Saddle Horse Breeders Association in 1891. Its conformation has probably become finer and showier, and more emphasis is now placed on animated action than upon comfortable riding. Many heavier American Saddle Horses are trained for showing in the Fine Harness classes. Still, those American Saddle Horses which do not conform exactly to show standards are generally found to be fine riding animals, and have been accepted into nearly all equine areas in which saddle horses are found — as hunters and jumpers, pleasure and trail horses, and even sometimes as utility horses in the western part of the United States. They have been used in the capacity of upgrading other breeds, also, helping to form the Missouri Fox Trotter, adding style to the Morgan, and probably contributing anonymously to many of the older breeds which listed miscellaneous riding blood in their lineages. The American Saddle Horse is frequently crossed on all kinds of ponies to create Five-gaited or Kentucky Saddlebred Ponies. These ponies are not a breed, but are crossbreds. They are shown in the Saddle Horse Division in special Five-gaited Pony classes at major horse shows, and command ex-

cellent sale prices, sometimes as high as ten thousand dollars.

The processes endured by the American Saddle Horse under preparation for showing are phenomenal. The breed is divided into two sections — the five-gaited horse, often called simply the Gaited Horse, and the three-gaited horse, often called the Walking Horse. The division is based entirely on the ability of the horse to perform certain gaits, and the amount of training it has had. The Walk-trot, which can do only the walk, trot, and canter, is not as highly valued as the Gaited Horse that can do those three gaits plus one fast and one slow artificial gait.

The rack is the fast gait, and is very difficult and tiring for the horse to perform. It is a three-beat gait sometimes called the single-foot, and the rhythm of the hoofbeats is evenly spaced and staccato. The slow gaits are numerous and the choice is up to the trainer and the ability of the horse, as well as the current preference in the show ring. They include the stepping pace, also called the slow pace and the amble (a broken, slow pace with a slight interval between hooves hitting the ground on the same side), the fox-trot (described in the Missouri Fox Trotter section), and the running walk (described in the Tennessee Walking Horse section). The most popular slow gait at present is the stepping pace.

To indicate immediately the difference between the Gaited Horse and the Walk-trot Horse to the spectator, the horses are fitted differently. The Gaited Horse has a long, full tail and mane, whereas the Walk-trot Horse has the upper nine inches of its tail either clipped or pulled and has a roached mane. Both are often completely clipped over the entire body to facilitate grooming and give a trim appearance.

The operation of turning an American Saddle Horse into a show horse is an endless job begun when the animal is quite young. With the aid of Novocain, the depressor muscles at the base of the tail are cut, and from that day forward the horse must wear what is called a tail-set harness during the show season. The tail-set consists of a girth band with a long strap leading along the spine to the tail, where it is tightly cinched to pull the tail straight up and prevent the cut muscles from growing together again. In some states, cutting is illegal, and breeders in these states have found that if the tail-set harness is applied early enough the cutting isn't necessary. The harness is taken off before the animal enters the ring, and an irritating powder called ginger is inserted into the anus to make the horse hold its tail even higher if possible. The ginger is rinsed out after showing. Most horse admirers deplore these tactics.

The tail of the Gaited Horse, in its prominent position, is the subject of quite a lot of acknowledged fakery. The natural hair is often dyed for showing to make it a more contrasting or showy color. Some horses do not have particularly long or thick tail hair, and upon these horses are usually fastened tail wigs and switches. The wigs are made of horse hair, sometimes gathered from the horse's stall, but artificial hair is becoming more popular. It is fastened to a strip of leather and tied to the base of the upright tail, where it flows over the crest and down nearly to the ground. For horses that do not need quite so much aid, there are hair switches which are knotted to the horse's natural hair near the end of the dock. Neither wig nor switch is detectable, even after a vigorous workout, if it is made and applied skillfully.

Breeders are quite particular about the handling of the mane and tail. Between shows, the tail is knotted or looped to prevent tangling, and the tail and mane are never brushed or combed. Instead, the groom patiently separates each strand from the next, applying a light coat of oil to each hair by running it through oiled fingers. This makes it shiny and helps to prevent tangles. After being groomed, the Gaited Horse's forelock has a ribbon braided into it, and there are three long ribbons, each a different color, braided into the upper part of the mane, falling on the off side with the rest of the mane. Oil is also massaged onto the nose and lips to make them pliable and lustrous, much improving the appearance of the horse.

The long, slim neck is one of the identifying marks of the American Saddle Horse. Unfortunately, now and then a Gaited Horse has a trifle meatier neck than is desirable. To make it appear fine and thinner, the mane is roached or hogged for as much as eight inches behind the ears.

Very special attention is paid to the horse's hooves. Since they are grown quite long to increase the action (toe weight affects the length of stride, and heel weight provides higher knee action) they are prone to breakage and splitting. Plastic and plastic wood fillers are often used to fortify and repair hooves, and reasonably close examination will reveal that many horses wear metal bands about three-fourths of an inch wide around one or more hooves as a brace against splitting or to protect a repaired hoof. Chains are sometimes fastened around the ankles to induce higher stepping.

Patience must be a hallmark of the American Saddle Horse.

It must be forbearing to endure such endless ministrations, but older horses sometimes come to enjoy all the attention. It must be somewhat bewildering, then, for a coddled show horse to be retired to grass that it has never tasted before in a pasture surrounded by fences that just might, conceivably, snarl its tail or scratch its pampered hide.

through stages of "A Palouse horse," "Apalouse horse," and finally, "Appaloosie" and "Appaloosa."

Similar oddly marked horses have been known in Europe and Asia for many thousands of years. Prehistoric cave drawings in France show tan ponies covered with black spots, and although it cannot be proven, these profusely spotted ponies might well have been drawn from life by the cave dwellers. Ancient Chinese drawings depicted ponies with Appaloosa spots, and ponies with Appaloosa patterns are found in Mongolia and Russia to this very day.

The advent of white settlers into the West visited upon the Nez Percé Indians the usual curse. By 1860 the homesteaders had broken the sod and established their farms with the use of heavy draft horses. Naturally enough, many a cumbersome mare succumbed to the persuasions of the lithe spotted stallions and either ran off with them or produced spindly, weedy foals, much to the settlers' chagrin. In addition, the tradition-bound missionaries disapproved of the races and sports continually indulged in by their potential converts. They felt that the horses were a bad influence on the Indians, giving them too much freedom to roam and wealth, for the Indian's worth among his peers was determined by the number of horses he had. These self-centered white squatters, the missionaries and the settlers, prevailed upon the government to put the Nez Percé under strict control. When the Nez Percé rebelled against being torn from their homeland and being placed on a reservation, their horses were seized and either killed outright or driven away so that the Indians had no way to fight and were eventually subdued. Their spotted war ponies were

drastically reduced in numbers, and those that were left mostly fell into the hands of ignorant drovers or farmers and were carelessly bred. It is amazing that they have managed the comeback that they have.

The Appaloosa of today is not by any means the spotted horse stock that once existed, for there have been large infusions of Arabian, Quarter Horse, and several other breeds. But the Appaloosa Horse Club, formed in 1938, has set definite goals of conformation and type so that it seems likely that the time will come when the Appaloosa will be distinguishable by its conformation as well as its color pattern. That goal is partially reached now. However, many Appaloosas today are bred for their racing qualities, often beng crossed with speedy Quarter Horses or Thoroughbreds. These horses have more the look of spotted Thoroughbreds than spotted stock horses, and there will probably always be a split in opinion as to what constitutes the perfect Appaloosa, depending upon whether the person arguing is a racing fan or a stock horse enthusiast.

Racing is big business to many Appaloosa breeders. Some of the largest tracks have now opened to Appaloosas and they race under pari-mutuel betting, making some excellent times and adding to the excitement with their bright markings. It has become a regulation that all entries must be tatooed on the lip with a permanent number to insure proper identification.

Great pains have been taken to make sure that every horse is correctly identified in its registration papers. On the back of the certificate there are several photographs of the horse, as well as a written description giving the type of pattern and the colors.

The typical patterns sometimes fall by the wayside since there are often admixtures of one or more patterns as well as occasional white face and leg markings. In addition to acceptable coat markings, the horse must also have white sclera encircling the eye; particolored skin on the nose, lips, and genital area; narrowly striped hooves; and a scanty mane and tail in order to be registered as an Appaloosa. Any indication of pony, draft, pinto, or albino breeding eliminates it at once, as do the presence of cryptorchids (undescended testicles) or a height of under 14 hands at maturity.

There are several other breeds which have Appaloosa markings but which are not Appaloosas. The most closely related is the Appaloosa Pony. Since the Appaloosa Horse Club bars any Appaloosa under 14 hands, there are sometimes Appaloosas with impeccable breeding which cannot qualify. These and other miscellaneous Appaloosa-type ponies may be registered with the National Appaloosa Pony Association. The Pony of the Americas is a breed with Appaloosa coloring, and the Colorado Rangerbred is often mistaken for the Appaloosa, sometimes the differences can only be found in their pedigrees.

The spots quite often present a strange appearance upon examination. Some are ringed by a shaded area, as if the spots had gotten wet and smeared or run; other spots are solid with a sharply delineated perimeter; and in the snowflake spot, there is just a concentrated scattering of hairs forming the shape. The shapes are varied, the four major types being the round or oval squaw marks, diamond-shaped spots, pear-shaped teardrops, and feather spots, long with blurred edges. When a spot occurs at the base of the mane hairs, the mane at that place is the color of the spot. On some horses with a series of spots along the crest, the mane appears to be striped like a zebra's. The spots can be felt with the fingers when the horse is in winter coat, for the dark hair grows at a different rate from the white hair. The mare Appaloosa is usually less colorfully marked than the stallion.

The Appaloosa Horse is shown in the western style with western gear. The mane is generally roached except for a handful at the withers, but the tail is left natural, for the Appaloosa is born with a "western tail," scanty and sparse, and it usually falls to just the right length.

The popularity of the Appaloosa has climbed high in the past twenty years, ranking it among the leaders in yearly registration of horses. The average price for a yearling is between five hundred and nine hundred dollars, but of course some of the yearlings with racing potential bring much higher prices.

The chief use of the Appaloosa is as a western utility and pleasure horse. As the Appaloosa has become more abundant, the market for poor specimens has decreased, so that new owners are usually pleased with their buys. They put their horses to any number of jobs, such as cutting, roping, parade use, and even English jumping sports with equal success.

Arabian

Outstanding points of conformation:

HEIGHT: 14:1 to 15:1.

COLORS AND MARKINGS: all solid colors, including dapple-gray and rose dapple. The bay and chestnut often show faint dappling, and, contrary to most literature, white spots often appear on the body, especially on the underline. White face and legs quite common.

FACE: is straight or concave (dished) below the eyes.

MUZZLE: is smaller than that of most other breeds.

EYES: are nearly always dark, and glass eyes are penalized in breeding classes.

EARS: are small and smaller on stallions than on mares.

NECK: is exceedingly arched on fine specimens.

MANE AND TAIL: mane and tail hair are fine and silky, not as thick as in other breeds. Tail is set high and arches gaily whenever the horse moves.

THERE IS SCARCELY any light horse breed that hasn't felt the direct or indirect influence of Arabian blood. Of the draft breeds, only the Percheron has Arabian breeding, and nearly all ponies except for some of the northernmost European ponies have a touch of Arabian blood. A cross to Arabian blood will revive the most despondent breed to new vigor in a few short generations, as well as improve its general style and beauty as no other breed can do.

The Arabian is an excellent horse, but it is no accident. Nearly four thousand years ago, the nomads of the Middle East were using horses. There is much controversy about what those horses looked like and from what they evolved. Some people contend that they were a distinct breed apart from the Tarpan and Przewalski's Horse, but there is little evidence to support this claim. They probably all came from the same ancient ancestor — wild and ugly — but while the descendants of the Tarpan and Przewalski's Horse had to shift for themselves, the Turkish, Persian, and Arab nomads were actively and carefully breeding their ponies to get a desired result. They bred for a beautiful head and crested neck, for a tail that flew like a banner, for a horse capable of epic feats, and for skin that was always black, regardless of the hair color. Only the most perfectly bred horses had the black skin, and the Arabs called them *keheilan,* a word derived from the Arabian word *kuhl,* meaning "eye shadow," for the dark skin showed around the eyes like heavily applied eye shadow. In time the term *keheilan* came to be synonymous with "purebred."

The desert nomads considered their horse to be a gift of the gods, a condensation of wind and flame. And in truth, the horse was a godsend to the Arabian, for without it and its special merits he could not have traveled or survived in the vast sandy reaches of the desert. Mares were the most highly treasured by the desert dwellers, and a horse's descent was traced through the dam's side, stallions being below notice and scorned. It is this fact that made importation of Arabian stallions to British and American soil so easy, whereas good mares were practically impossible to acquire. The mares were guarded fanatically, for it was felt that if any mare were to mate with a non-Arabian or even an Arabian horse of doubtful bloodlines, it would so taint her as to make her useless for further breeding. The reasoning was that she would pass on characteristics of the impure sire to future offspring, no matter how pure succeeding sires might be. This supposed phenomenon

was called telegony, and was swallowed whole by even well-educated Americans until about the first decade of this century, when exhaustive experiments finally dislodged the idea. It was because of this that some of the finest mares were gladly sold to eager foreign buyers while scheming Arabs laughed up their voluminous sleeves. Today, few good Arabian horses are left in their native land, the vast majority and best animals being found in North America.

The Arabs were extremely proud of their horses' fine profiles. They had a special term, *mitbah,* for the angle at which the neck meets the head; they called the bulging forehead and dished nose the *jibbah.* The *jibbah* was highly touted by some as a feature which obviously gave the Arabian horse more brain-room than other breeds, but examination of skulls has shown that most of the room is taken up by air space within the bones. Of course, all desert wanderers didn't have the same goals for their horses, and some tribes, particularly the Bedouins, were acknowledged to be the best horse breeders. As a result, there were many horses bred with perfectly straight profiles and other divergent conformations, some being severe faults. Some horses examined in the desert had such long pasterns that when they galloped, their fetlocks actually bumped the ground. Another fault was low, flat withers, which made it difficult to fit a saddle and keep it in place on the horse's back. Since tribesmen rode without stirrups, they disliked the trot, seldom used it, and never developed it in their horses. As a result, the Arabian horse has been noted for its poor trot. Most of these points are being improved upon or eliminated. There are two things about the Arabian's structure that make it a curiosity: it generally has one fewer back vertebrae than other horses, and two fewer tail vertebrae; sometimes it has no chestnuts on its hind legs and only small ones in front.

The desert people were nomads and fighters, and they marauded and warred and crossed entire countries in their raids. In the process, their horses sowed their seed across the Middle and Near East and eventually into Europe, upgrading native horses as they went. The Romans also acquired Arabian horses, and when all of Europe was under their dominance they took their horses with them wherever they went. During the Dark Ages in Europe, there was little horse breeding, but things began to pick up again in the sixteenth and seventeenth centuries. In the late 1600's, the British began to import "oriental horses" (this is a catch-all phrase for any horses from east of Europe or northern Africa), and it was at about this time that the controversy over the Barb began.

The Barb is a native horse of northern Africa. It is larger than the Arabian and a bit coarser, with low-set tail, undished nose, and hairy fetlocks. Some say it descended from the Arabian, but this is probably not true since there are indications that it has existed in Africa nearly as long as the Arabian has existed in Arabia. It is more likely that they both descended from the same general stock. The Godolphin stallion, one of the founders of the English Thoroughbred, wavers between Barb and Arabian status as the argument continues.

The Arabian horse is not a newcomer to America. It arrived in half-bred form along with the first imported English Thoroughbreds, and at about that time farseeing American horse breeders began to tour Arabia on horse-finding trips of their own. Since for many years there were only a limited number of Arabian horses in the United States, no one bothered to set up a registry for them. And since the American Thoroughbred was in its formative stages, breeding native mares to oriental stallions, the American Thoroughbred Stud Book registered them in a special Arabian section.

The Arabian horse of today is quite a bit larger than its forebears. In the desert, the horse seldom reached 15 hands, but now it often does, with some individuals topping 15 hands. Close inbreeding sometimes produces ponies as small as 12 hands.

The classic Arabian stallion with fine chiseled features, good *jibbah* and *mitbah,* and graceful form is an ideal only sometimes realized. The average Arabian has many of the features but not all, and some frequently found faults are a short bull neck, boxy face and straight profile, meaty, chunky body, and cow hocks. A saving grace of many an ordinary Arabian horse is its beautiful satiny coat which often, on bays and chestnuts, glistens with an iridescent rainbow luster in addition to the usual golden glint — a really amazing sight, and one not found among other breeds. The average Arabian horse usually has a good share of the characteristics which made its ancestors perfect desert cruisers. It can tolerate hot and cold temperatures, survive on little water, travel comfortably at high altitudes, get the maximum amount of nourishment from its feed, and travel long distances carrying as much as one-fourth its own weight. Its strong legs, large joints, and sturdy tendons make it less susceptible to leg ailments than most other breeds. All these traits make it one of America's best loved pleasure breeds.

While many Arabian horse breeders try to tell the public that the Arabian horse never has pinto markings, this is not so. White spots are often found on the body, usually on the underline, and such horses are duly registered although frowned upon in breeding stock. Aside from pinto coloration, the Arabian also possesses extraordinary pink or rose dapple color, a type of dapple-gray found sometimes on younger horses, making them positively purple. Unfortunately, this fades to white as the horse matures.

Chickasaw

Outstanding points of conformation:

HEIGHT: 13:1 to 14:3.
COLORS AND MARKINGS: bay, black, chestnut, gray, roan, sorrel, and palomino. White markings are common.
HEAD: short and blunt.
EARS: short.
NECK: exceedingly short.
HIPS: square and blocky.
PASTERN: short and strong.
MANE AND TAIL: tail is low-set, and both mane and tail are trimmed in the western fashion.

THE CHICKASAW HORSE has contributed substantially to the history of the American horse breeds, but it is perhaps one of the least known native breeds of horses in America today. Its history is long, going back to the 1500's when De Soto and his band of adventurers entered Florida with about two hundred horses and proceeded north into Tennessee and North Carolina. In their travels, they came across the Chickasaw Indians and spent some time among them, accepting their hospitality and kindnesses. But as usual in white-Indian relations, De Soto transgressed the bounds of courtesy by demanding that the Chickasaw bear his supplies and loads when the explorers were ready to move on. In righteous indignation, the insulted Chickasaw attacked the Spaniards and drove their horses off into the forest. This deplorable incident in human relations had fortunate equine results, however, for many of the escaped horses were later captured by the Indians, bred, and put to use.

The colonists who later came to settle in this area immediately recognized the worth of these Indian ponies, which were quite different from the stock they had brought with them. The Chickasaw animals were smaller, averaging in the pony range of 13 hands, and they were solid and very strong, fast-moving but better for short bursts of speed than for long-distance running. This suited the colonists admirably since in the semicleared forests there was seldom a place for a horse to stretch out in a long run. Through trade and barter, they obtained some from the Indians and began to breed them.

Crossed with the colonists' riding and utility stock to produce larger offspring, they began to develop into the horses which would later be used in the West for herding cattle, cutting, roping, and otherwise performing tasks that require catlike agility, fast thinking, short bursts of speed, and sturdy muscling. Even during that long-ago time, they were lauded as the finest utility horses to be found anywhere.

In colonial times, especially in the South, breeding records were kept quite regularly. However, when the Chickasaw's popularity began to wane in about 1800 with breeders more interested in Chickasaw-oriental crosses for racing and utility purposes, registrations were dropped and the pure Chickasaw was practically forgotten except by those people who used it daily and quietly appreciated it.

Interest has revived again, now, as it has with many ancient parent breeds. There seems to be a tendency in America these days to go back to the source, as can be seen by the popularity of the original-type mustangs and Morgans. In the isolated mountain regions where nearly pure breeding has been carried on for the last two hundred years, even without records, the Chickasaw is very popular. The breed registry, the Chickasaw Horse Association, has recently been reactivated and carries on a respectable traffic in registrations.

Although the Chickasaw is being crossbred with the Quarter Horse in a limited manner with some very fine results, it has earned admiration in its own right. A comparison with the Quarter Horse reveals some fundamental differences. The Chickasaw is often much smaller, with a height between 13:1 and 14:3 hands, whereas the Quarter Horse stands between 14 and 15 hands. The Chickasaw Horse has a flatter chest with the muscles on its shoulder coming higher, and also a shorter back. The head is shorter, as are the ears. On the Chickasaw Horse, the pasterns are short and the legs are somewhat crooked, allowing it to get its feet well under it for faster starts. The Quarter Horse is sometimes crooked-legged, but not to this extent. The most outstanding characteristic is the very short neck of the Chickasaw. It is so extremely short that the horse must bend its front leg in order to reach the grass it must eat. This would seem to be more of a handicap than an attribute; but it must be kept in mind that a short, strong neck is particularly suited to a mountain horse, for it permits it to climb and lift its forehand with much less fatigue than a long-necked horse. To bear this out, the Chickasaw is much prized as a backcountry horse, where it must travel in brushy, steep areas and fight its way through swampy lowlands.

The Chickasaw Horse proves its mettle in the rodeo arena, also, in such fields as dogging, calf roping, and barrel racing.

It might be interesting to keep an eye on the Chickasaw Horse, for it shows promise of regaining the reputation of an all-round fine utility and using horse that it had acquired in colonial times. Although competition is tougher now, it is partly due to the Chickasaw Horse's influence that this is so. It would be good to see this plucky little horse become well known once again.

Galiceño

Outstanding points of conformation:

HEIGHT: 12 to 13:2 hands.

COLORS AND MARKINGS: solid colors including brown, chestnut, gray, roan, buckskin, dun, sorrel, black, and bay, but no albinos or pintos. White markings common.

FORELEGS: quite muscular, approaching that of the Quarter Horse.

CROUP: is not level, slopes slightly.

REAR LEGS: are found slightly more under the horse than usual.

MANE AND TAIL: are clipped in the western style in the United States.

THE GALICEÑO (pronounced Gal-i-seen-yo) is a relative newcomer to the United States. Some of the first to appear here were discovered in Mexico in 1958 by an American tourist, who immediately brought one back with him. Shortly after that, more importations were made by horsemen who recognized their excellent points and reached the conclusion that they had found a pony-sized horse that could meet the demands of both children and adults alike.

Although the Galiceño is new here, it is an old breed. It has lived on the coastal areas of Mexico since the Conquistadores abandoned its ancestors there, having used them to clean out Mexican silver lodes. Part of the horses thus discarded drifted north and formed the original herds of mustangs, while many

roamed south to become the Argentinian Criollo. But a portion of them stayed in Mexico, for they were caught by the native Indians and put to work for them, packing and pulling. Due to their isolated range, the Galiceño (so named because it is thought to have come from the province Galicia in Spain) did not have occasion to outcross, and might be considered one of the more pure breeds descending from the original Spanish Barbs and Jennets brought by the Spaniards to the New World.

The Spanish Jennet was esteemed for its easy paces, and this trait has survived in the Galiceño, for it performs four gaits: the walk, trot, canter, and a fast, rhythmical running walk. The Mexicans regarded their Galiceños highly, especially appreciating their versatility as riding horses, cart haulers, and pack horses. They used them in the mountains, for they are cautious on rough trails and sure-footed under even the most adverse conditions.

The small size is probably an indication of the size of the original Spanish horses. Although the Galiceño is technically a pony, from 12 to 13:2 hands, it is also a western horse, and has no pony breeding. In addition, its action and style are those of a full-sized horse, so it is usually classed with the horses instead of the ponies. It is small enough for children to ride, but adults don't feel oversize on it.

The Galiceño is most likely of the same general stock as the Paso Fino. But the Paso Fino has been increased in size through generous doses of Arabian, Morgan, and American Saddle Horse, so that its natural style (which was probably much like the Galiceño's originally) has been improved or at least changed.

Most importations of Galiceños have been made into the West and Canada. The registry and a considerable number of animals are in the state of Washington. In the United States, it is shown in western style with the mane roached and the tail pulled so that it falls to about the hocks. In Canada, the mane and tail are usually left untrimmed and unthinned. It does seem a shame to cut them since they are especially long, full, and fine.

Galiceños seem to take naturally to such western uses as cutting, roping, and general ranch work. They have great stamina and can carry an adult-size rider a full day without fatigue. However, in making the Galiceño into a western horse, it is possible that its natural running walk may be shoved into the background. Although the Galiceño is firmly entrenched in the United States, it does not yet have sufficient numbers to command its own shows, and events except in a minor way, and the beautiful and comfortable running walk does not get the notice it deserves.

Having been developed by hard-working family-oriented Mexican owners, the Galiceño has naturally been bred for even disposition and easy handling. It shows unusual gentleness, even after a rough ride or a difficult training period or workout. It is this trait that makes the Galiceño an excellent family horse as well as the perfect working horse for games or rodeo.

In conformation, the Galiceño is a rather light breed. Its build is smooth and lithe, and the muscles are plentiful but fine. Its hind legs are a trifle more crooked than most breeds, putting its feet well under the body. The shortness of its back gives it great weight-carrying ability.

This little horse is likely to become a familiar sight in all fields, for it lends itself well to such uses as jumping, driving, parade, gymkhana, and trail riding, as well as very enjoyable and (especially at the running walk) exciting pleasure riding.

Hackney

Outstanding points of conformation:

HEIGHT: 14:2 to 16 hands. Horse is heavy in proportion to height.
COLORS AND MARKINGS: chestnut, brown, and bay are most usual, but black, and roan are also seen. White markings common.
SHOULDERS: heavy and well muscled.
BACK: very broad.
MANE AND TAIL: tail is docked, mane is pulled.

IT IS, perhaps, impractical and misleading to include the Hackney Horse in a list of horses commonly found in America today. Its numbers have steadily decreased along with its usefulness until few are to be found anymore. But the Hackney Horse has an honorable lineage, and was one of the more important types of horse in the United States during the country's formative years, for it drew carriages and transports in great numbers, and it deserves at least a mention.

The Hackney comes in two sizes, large and small. The Hackney Pony is a fairly recent development in the show world, an offshoot from the larger horse, and has found favor as a harness pony. There are a few Hackney Horses left, and one of their primary uses is to provide stock from which Hackney Ponies come.

The Hackney Horse is a harness horse, well known for its brilliant, high-reaching action at both the trot and the walk. It has

been around, in one form or another, for several hundred years, originating in the Great Horse of Belgium, from which descended the draft horses and the Norfolk Trotter, an English harness horse of heavy build. The Norfolk Trotter was crossed with Shales 699, a great-great-grandson of the Darley Arabian. Shales's sire Blaze was a Thoroughbred, and among his get were Messenger, a famous Standardbred sire, and Herod, of well-known racing fame. This blood gave class and dash to an otherwise ordinary utility horse and eventually helped, with a bit of Norwegian Pony breeding for speed and stamina, to create a breed that has seldom been matched for fire and sparkle at the trot.

As with most utility horses, the advent of the railroad, then in immediate succession the automobile, truck, and bus, nearly extinguished the demand for harness horses. The motorized conveyances could go nearly anywhere a horse and buggy or cart could go (despite early cries of "Get a horse!") and could do it a great deal faster.

The Hackney arrived in America in 1822 by way of the Standardbred foundation sire Bellfounder. Another Hackney, Fireaway, was imported from England later, and these two were used on native mares to produce excellent harness horses although they were not promoted as Hackneys. Later importations swelled the ranks of the Hackney type, and eventually, in 1891 the American Hackney Horse Society was organized.

Speed and endurance were important Hackney attributes. Speeds of seventeen miles per hour were not uncommon, and twenty-four miles per hour was recorded for shorter distances. The style and conformation became fixed as the breed matured, the average horse being powerfully built, big, broad, and short-legged, with an intelligent head, fine neck, and perfect shoulders. The original Hackneys didn't have the exaggerated high step — instead they were known for their long, strong stride. When they caught the attention of the city coachmen, there came a demand for matched pairs with very high action, and in short order this became the rule rather than the exception. It is still in evidence to this day.

Bays, chestnuts, browns, and blacks have always been the most popular, and these are nearly the only colors to be found today. Around the turn of the century, roan and buckskin were also in favor.

The Hackney Horse has never had very wide distribution in the United States. Even at the peak of its usefulness it was only seen in the eastern and north-central portions of the country. And it is there, mostly, that its descendants can be found, although the Hackney Ponies are more evenly distributed. The Hackney Horse is used mostly in the show ring in its pure state, and a tendency to produce good hunters and jumpers has caused it to be successfully crossed with Thoroughbreds for use as medium- and heavyweight hunters. It was a popular cavalry mount in World War I.

No one can predict the future of the Hackney Horse. It may regain its popularity, or it may go the way of the other old coach horses and quietly disappear.

Lipizzan

Outstanding points of conformation:

HEIGHT: 15 to 16 hands.
COLORS AND MARKINGS: most are gray, which turns to white, but sometimes a bay
appears, and on occasion, a chestnut or roan.
HEAD: big, sometimes convex (roman-nosed).
EARS: small for size of head.
NECK: very strong, sometimes even heavy, but well proportioned.
SHOULDERS: heavy and muscular.
LEGS: short and strong, with prominent joints and tendons.
QUARTERS: strong, gracefully rounded.
MANE AND TAIL: hair is fine and thick, if left its natural length and thickness.

THE LIPIZZAN or Lipizzaner horse of Austria is probably the best known horse in the world. It is a wingless Pegasus, flying where no other horses fly, performing movements on the ground seldom perfected by other horses, and movements above the ground that no other horse has ever accomplished through training. It is royalty, irreproachable, and one of the most beautiful horses this world has ever known.

The most interesting thing about the movements or figures it performs is that not one of them is unnatural in its execution; for a playful horse turned loose and free into a pasture with companions sometimes performs unselfconsciously similar gymnastics without any special thought or training at all. The Lipizzan is fascinating to watch, equally rewarding and satisfying to the seasoned horseman who knows what training must have gone into each effortlessly done but difficult movement, and to the businessman who has never sat a horse.

Because some excellent Lipizzan stock has begun to appear in America, and since some serious breeding and training is being carried on by those people fortunate enough to have acquired a Lipizzan, it might be interesting to look into the history and training of these magnificent horses and discuss what their future in the United States might be.

For two hundred years the Spanish Riding School has trained the Lipizzan with methods which haven't changed much since their introduction in 1735. These methods and aids were formulated slowly and carefully with the Lipizzan horse in mind, and it is obvious that it would be difficult to improve on the final performance in any way. The Lipizzan of today is the result of a combination in the early 1700's of the heavy-set Kladruber horse of Spanish and Neapolitan breeding, crossed with the little northern Italian horse, with later additions of Arabian blood. This mixture created a heavy-boned, elegantly formed horse, with greatly developed hindquarters and shoulders, an almost delicate head often showing much Arabian breeding, and a graceful and dignified attitude. The color is nearly always a gray which will turn white, although bays and chestnuts are occasionally seen. The stallions chosen for training are usually white although one bay stallion was used by the Lipizzaner troupe that toured America in 1964. The foals that will later be white are born black and lighten with age.

The Lipizzan is very slow to mature, and the foals run free until they are four years old, then enter a two-year initial breaking period. Each horse has its own trainer and no one else ever touches it. Several years of training in figures on the ground, such as the *piaffe* (a springy trot performed without forward movement), the *passage* (the *piaffe* done with forward movement), the *passade* (a turn on the haunches), and many others, determine whether the stallion is capable of working above the ground, performing the *levade* (in which it balances perfectly still on its hind legs for as long as fifteen seconds), the *courbette* (the horse makes several leaps on its hind legs, with the forefeet never touching the ground), the *capriole* (during which the Lipizzan goes into a *levade*, then springs into the air and lashes out with its hind legs; this progression may be repeated), and other movements and combinations of movements.

The riders wear European costumes designed in the 1700's, including bicorn hats, formal coats with tails, and long, black boots; the horses are strangely gárbed, too, in old-fashioned Old World tack. To see the troupe in action is an exciting experience impossible to describe, and the appearance of the Lipizzaner troupe here, as well as a Walt Disney movie about them, and at least one best-selling novel that centered around them and the Spanish Riding School, were partly responsible for the recent upsurge of interest in the breed in the United States.

The Spanish Riding School nearly perished in World War II, but was saved through the efforts of General George Patton, and reestablished later. When the war was over, Patton brought many of the horses back with him as war booty. Some other Lipizzaners were later imported privately and a registry was begun around 1950, but it fell inactive and much pure Lipizzan stock was dispersed and pedigrees were lost. Fortunately, interest has again revived, and the spirited white horses are finding a new home in America.

They are sometimes seen in circuses and in dressage events at horse shows, and their owners are finding out that the Lipizzan makes a magnificent riding horse and hunter. Although America will probably never have a riding school comparable to Vienna's, some American trainers are elatedly getting extraordinary results with these graceful white stallions, the Lipizzaners.

Missouri Fox Trotter

Outstanding points of conformation:

HEIGHT: 14 to 16 hands.
COLORS AND MARKINGS: all colors, including pinto and albino. Sorrel is the most common, and white markings are often seen.
BODY: especially deep and well ribbed for a saddle horse.

THE MISSOURI FOX TROTTER is a well-built animal, resembling nothing so much as an ordinary utility horse. Its uniqueness lies in its ability to execute the strange gait known as the fox-trot. In horse shows, the fox-trot is considered one of the slow gaits, along with the running walk and the slow or stepping pace. Most horsemen describe it as a gait in which the horse trots with its back feet and walks with its front feet (we must assume that it is a slow trot and a fast walk; otherwise it would trip over itself). The fox-trot has been called a loose-jointed trot, a dogtrot, and a "shog," the last name perhaps being a contraction of the words shuffle and jog. But walking and trotting at the same time is difficult to visualize, and a more technical description is: the horse hits the ground with its hind foot shortly before the diagonal forefoot lands. With each step, the horse nods its head and may flop its ears. Since the gait is not a high-stepping one, it gives a smooth

ride and is quite sure-footed. For this reason, the Missouri Fox Trotter makes a fine pleasure and using horse, and gives quite a comfortable trail ride, achieving speeds of between five and ten miles per hour.

The fox-trot isn't exactly an inherited gait, nor is it a natural gait. It must be taught, and this is done by putting the horse into a flat-footed walk then crowding it into a faster speed while at the same time holding it back from the trot. Sooner or later, the horse learns what is required and will naturally fall into the gait on command. However, it is a difficult gait to learn, and the Missouri Fox Trotter seems to learn it more easily than most breeds. This inborn tendency is not unusual in the horse world — it is well known that whereas many years ago Standardbreds had to be taught to pace, many foals of recent generations pace naturally from birth. It may be that in time the Fox Trotter will have inherited the ability to perform this gait naturally.

The Missouri Fox Trotter is an old breed in some respects, although the registry has only been in operation since 1948. The ancestors of the Fox Trotter were horses of Arabian, Morgan, and plantation lineage brought to the Ozark hills of Arkansas and Missouri from Kentucky, Tennessee, and Virginia about a hundred years ago by migrating settlers. Later on, American Saddle Horse,

Standardbred, and Tennessee Walking Horse blood were added to improve form and disposition. All records and the stud book of the Missouri Fox Trotting Breed Association were destroyed by fire in 1958, but the registry was immediately reincorporated and has experienced steady growth since then. It is still partly open to foundation stock, and any horse with one registered parent may be registered.

The breed is not yet standardized in conformation. The various breeders have not had identical goals for a long enough time to have created a distinct look. In general, the horse is sturdier than most riding breeds, more along the lines of the Tennessee Walking Horse than any other. It has had a large infusion of that blood, and the standards for both breeds are nearly the same.

The Fox Trotter is always ridden with western gear. A great deal of wisdom is shown in the ruling that no artificial trappings such as tail wigs, set tails, tie downs, special shoes, or braces may be used. This is evidently a move designed to save the breed from the unfortunate state of some breeds which are used chiefly as show horses and are encumbered with all sorts of sophisticated constraints to make them seem to be what they are not.

The Missouri Fox Trotter is designed more for useful service than for anything else. Besides being a good show horse, it excels in endurance and trail rides and has been used for working cattle and for other ranch uses, as well as working for the Forest Service. It is such a gentle horse that it makes an ideal family horse.

Its colors include all shades found among horses, with a predominance of chestnuts with white markings. Palominos are liberally represented, and although some reluctance is shown by the registry, pinto and spotted horses are allowed if they have good quality.

Morgan

Outstanding points of conformation:

HEIGHT: 14:1 and 15:1 hands. Body tends toward stockiness.
COLORS AND MARKINGS: bays and chestnuts most frequent; also seen are black, brown, and occasionally palomino. White markings are common, but small and not above the knee or hock.
EYES: walleyes are not permitted.
HEAD: short and wide, bones neat and well defined.
FACE: profile is flat or slightly dished.
MUZZLE: small and neat.
NECK: is shorter than most breeds, has good crest.
CANNONS: are extremely short.
FEET: are small.
CROUP: is sloped and slightly rounded.
MANE AND TAIL: are full and long, left that way for showing.
FEATHER: more than in most other light breeds, but this is removed for showing.

IT WOULD BE INTERESTING and perhaps quite revealing to go back in time to colonial Vermont and settle the question once and for all about Justin Morgan's little bay stallion Figure. There is argument about his birthdate and place, his ancestors, just when, and how, he died. Since nearly every reference gives different information, and apparently no one knows for sure, it is difficult to know what to believe. But a careful sifting of data and elimination of unlikely or impossible claims leaves a probable trail of events as follows.

A small, dark bay of unknown ancestry was foaled in Massachusetts or Vermont between the years of 1789 and 1793. Shortly after, he became the property of a singing Welsh schoolteacher named Justin Morgan, who received him in payment for a debt either before or after he moved from Massachusetts to Vermont. Figure was a tiny stallion, barely 14 hands high, but he immediately began to earn his way, being rented by Justin to farmers for clearing logs off wooded farmland. Justin Morgan had suffered from tuberculosis for several years, and when he died in 1798 his horse, which had won a reputation for his trotting speed, strength, level-headedness, and intelligence, was sold to a logger and began a long life of owner-to-owner existence. During his travels with at least ten owners, he stood at stud innumerable times for trifling sums of two to five dollars (unknown to Figure's owners, Sherman, a son of Figure, was drawing mares at twenty to fifty dollars each) and his get, mostly with his markings and conformation despite the type of mare, began to make themselves felt on the trotting tracks throughout the East. While Figure was sought out as a sire because he was sure to turn out good offspring, his reputation was limited to the people who had seen him work or admired his style. None of the farmers guessed that the proud little stallion pulling the peddler's cart, the plow, the Conestoga wagon, or the big logs, was founding a new breed of horses someday to be known as Morgan Horses. In fact, it wasn't until the mid-1800's that the preponderance of excellent, nearly identical bay horses with speed, stamina, and willingness started a furor of curiosity and speculation about their origin. By then, only sales slips and memories could bring back the story of a stallion that had died of neglect almost thirty years before.

People being prone to exaggerate, and memories being known to dim with time, the various stories are naturally different and

sometimes a little embroidered here and there. But they all agreed on his appearance. They told of a dark bay stallion with glossy, wavy black mane and tail, small and short-legged, with a proudly crested neck and fine head. He was courageous and docile, with vigorous constitution and a gay bearing. His chest was broad and deep, his legs well knit and sinewy, which made possible his stylish square trot and quick springy step. Figure was compact, the graybeards said, with muscle to spare and a strong, short back, and he couldn't have weighed more than about nine hundred pounds. He wasn't drafty, though, no sir, not a sign of draft horse in him. And when he matched trotting speed with all comers, the old-timers smiled to remember, his head was high and proud, and he mostly won all the races. Yes, the old men gave him quite an accolade, and they all agreed on what he looked like, no matter how different their stories about his prowess and origin.

It was the fast trot of Figure's descendants that almost caused the undoing of the Morgan breed in the 1850's. In an effort to make them faster and better able to compete with the Standard-bred Hambletonians, some breeders began to split away and di-lute their Morgans with Thoroughbred, Standardbred, and other racing blood until the Morgan type was almost completely sub-merged. Most of this hybrid split was ultimately absorbed by the Standardbred, and undoubtedly contributed a great deal of good blood to that breed. Unfortunately, some of the hybrids re-joined the Morgan family, bringing their mixed blood with them. Many Morgan breeders managed to keep their stock pure while lending blood to help form the American Saddle Horse, Tennessee Walking Horse, and the Quarter Horse breeds. Several years later, as if the initial diluting of bloodlines with Standardbred blood weren't enough, many Morgan breeders decided that if the Standardbred had the trotting field, the Morgan should take over the saddle horse realm. Since the American Saddle Horse was already well established (admittedly with former help from the Morgans) the Morgan breeders tried to infuse American Saddle Horse blood into the Morgan line. This still further weakened the Morgan strain without giving it a significant role as The Perfect Saddle Horse. The result of mating chunky, short-legged, muscu-lar Morgans to streamlined, graceful, lightweight American Saddle Horses produced generally horrible mismatched messes resem-bling neither. In the nick of time, some Morgan breeders began to recognize the usefulness of the pure Morgan as an all-around horse, and they brought it intact through the difficult period when the automobile was becoming common. The drop in numbers was still almost disastrous. It was estimated in 1870 that 90 per-cent of the horses used in the cities and countryside for pulling carriages, railway streetcars, and coaches were Morgans. Only the backing of the United States Remount Service and the hand-ful of breeders maintained the Morgans until people realized that cars are nice but horses still have a place in the world.

The Morgan Horse has always been a favorite cavalry horse. During the Civil War it was considered the most desirable horse to be mounted upon. Even during World War I the call for Mor-gans was high, the fine stallion General Gates 666 being named the best sire for endurance horses and used extensively by the Remount Service for the production of cavalry mounts. Today the Morgan is used quite a lot as a police horse because of its calmness, equanimity, and graceful carriage, as well as its standard dark color.

It is seen more and more often at horse shows (sometimes unshod) in dressage, hunting and jumping, trotting races, carriage classes, and in special Justin Morgan performance classes, in which each entry performs under saddle, trots, races, and pulls a sledge piled high with boulders. There is an unfortunate trend these days, however, to apply to the show Morgan all the fitting and showing gimmicks once reserved for the American Saddle Horse. Its strong, sturdy feet are grown to injurious lengths (as much as seven or eight inches long) and its proud, free, normal action is encouraged to go higher and higher with less and less forward movement. The saddle seat is often of the sort that puts the rider far back on the horse's back (which not only looks terrible, but gives a jolting ride and is hard on the horse). And the Morgan is made to pose like a rocking horse, stretched as tight as a guitar string. One would think the lesson had been learned several years ago when the Morgan breeders tried to make the Morgan into a saddle horse and failed miserably. But perhaps the lesson must be driven home again to this several-times-removed generation of breeders and trainers of Morgan Horses.

Outside of horse shows, the Morgan has become well loved as a reliable saddle horse, hunter, trail and endurance horse, and polo pony — not fancy, but completely dependable. Some western horse shows feature cutting classes, and in recent years it has become commonplace to see Morgans earning their keep handsomely as cow horses on cattle ranches.

What makes the Morgan so good? There is much conjecture about his ancestors — everything from Thoroughbred and Arabian to British cavalry horse, Chickasaw Horse, and Narragansett Pacer have been suggested. Chances are, he had a little bit of all of them in his makeup. But his excellence stemmed from himself alone and from his amazing genetic ability to produce sons and daughters resembling himself and with his abilities time after time. Has any other light horse without a pedigree and carefully chosen parents ever done that — before or since?

Mustang

Outstanding points of conformation:

HEIGHT: no limits, but usually between 13 and 15 hands.
COLORS AND MARKINGS: all colors, including pinto and albino, and white markings very common. Duns and roans especially common.
FACE: usually straight or roman-nosed.
BODY: sometimes stunted by lack of good feed, muscles usually very tough and stringy; in general, wiry and strong.
HOOVES: very tough and enduring.

WRITERS about the Old West didn't write their tales for westerners. They wrote for the city dweller who had never seen a cowboy, a six-gun, or a mustang. If they ran short of authentic material, they blithely conjured up their own — admittedly more exciting but often far from the truth. It is not so surprising, then, that mustangs are commonly believed to have been magnificent creatures with high arched necks, heroic stature, and possessing those attributes more commonly seen in dogs or other best friends (i.e. faithfulness, fetching ability, etc.). They are pictured as silver, ebony, and other unusual colors, and the stallion is generally leading his band of mares and foals at a gallop away from danger. It is really too bad to have to find the truth elsewhere, but a careful look at the mustang's history will quickly point out the shortcomings of the myths.

The forerunners of the mustangs were the horses transported by Cortez from Spain for the purpose of conquering the western hemisphere and its inhabitants. There is dispute about whether or not his horses were of the highest grade. The Queen of Spain probably intended for him to have the best, but some authorities suspect that the sailors who were in charge of the horses sold the good ones before leaving Spain, replacing them with cheap nags, and pocketed the difference. Whatever the case, the average Spanish horse of that time was only pony size, standing roughly 14 hands. It was short-legged and short-backed, and had a hearty constitution, which is the only reason it managed to get to the New World, for the trip took two to three months and losses among the ponies were sometimes as high as 50 percent.

When the survivors reached their destination, they helped to conquer the Aztecs, who incidently couldn't have been so easily squashed if it hadn't been for those horses. They thought that the man-horse combination was a long-awaited god, and of course they could not raise arms against a god! For further conquering purposes, royal horse breeding farms were set up in the islands of Santo Domingo, Puerto Rico, Jamaica, and Cuba. As the new crops of horses were taken to the mainland by the soldiers, they had many opportunities to escape: by exiting from ill-made corrals, wandering off while grazing, and by being stolen by curious Indians. The Mexican Indians had an advantage over the Aztecs, who had been taken by surprise by the Conquistadores. They watched the Spaniards from hidden places and observed that the horses were not one-half of a god, but just animals like deer or coyotes, and the Indians were much impressed with the freedom of movement the horse gave the silver-coated men. By the time the sixteenth century had begun in America, the Indians of Mexico had become mobile. They used their horses to much better advantage than the Spaniards did. Mane and tail

hair was braided into hair ropes, and a shampoo in horse's blood was guaranteed to increase the shampooer's strength. A dead horse was almost as much good as a live horse, for it could be eaten; its hide was useful for all sorts of things such as making clothing, leggings, tents, and even saddles for riding live horses. But the Indian was just as careless as the white man with his steed, and soon feral herds were running wild and free to the south and to the north as years went by. The ones that went south became Criollos, but those that went north into the Great Plains of the American West were called mustangs.

They were joined by horses which De Soto had lost and abandoned, by strays stolen or strayed from Spanish Missions and land holdings, and later on by Indian ponies which had traveled west with Indians who had once lived in the eastern part of the United States, but who had been pushed out by the growing numbers of hostile white men. The meeting of former colonial ponies added quite a different type of blood, and although through generations of hardship the little mustang had somewhat degenerated from its original Spanish ancestors, this tended to coarsen its blood. When the white man himself finally came west, he brought along more cold-blooded horses in the form of utility horses and sometimes even heavy draft horses.

The mid-1800's saw the mustangs, as well as the Indians, fighting a losing battle to remain on their old ranges. The little horses, which had formerly been bay, brown, sorrel, dun, and pinto, began to show conspicuous numbers of dapple-gray and black, for the Percherons turned out to graze on the range were not slow to join the wild bands. Along with their color, they also transmitted their ungainly shape, so useful for farming and so ludicrous for a wild horse. The resulting offspring were heavy, with big feet and large heads, but little else to commend them, as a rule. Some horses of good breeding were also lost to the wild bands, but this, too, had a detrimental effect on the feral herds, for the farmers and ranchers, up in arms about the equine theft of their good stock, took to the plains and mountains to round up the mustangs and reclaim their horses. Sometimes the captured bands were sorted for branded animals and turned loose, but usually the ranchers killed the stallion of the herd to make their work easier, and after extracting the best stock either shot the mares and foals on the excuse that they ate too much grass and muddied the water holes, or they kept them and broke them for their remudas. Many ineptly broken mustangs ended up in rodeos.

Some herds of the Southwest managed to avoid the cattlemen fairly well, and remained mostly pure due to the vast spaces they roamed and the infrequency of their sallies into man-held territory. The safety and ability of the mustang band to avoid dangerous situations was as much the responsibility of some wise old mare as of the leading stallion. The phrase "leading stallion" is inappropriate in the sense that it was the old mare, wise in the ways of the country, that always led the band when it retreated from danger. It was the stallion that busied himself nipping the heels and rumps of laggards and stragglers, for it was important that the bunch stay together and travel its fastest. So, despite the glorious tales of the stallion leading his band, it just wasn't true.

The mustang managed to hold onto its freedom for a long time, but it was no match for grain-fed horses and wily cowboys who set out to catch it, for the cowboy switched to fresh horses when his mounts grew tired. So the mustang served as a cow horse (it was an excellent mount if broken intelligently), plow and utility horse, and finally, as dog food and fertilizer. This disgraceful fact will always be a blot on the history of the West. In addition to being run by cowboys on well-fed horses, mustangs were also chased with dogs, rifles, and finally planes and helicopters. They ran gamely until they dropped, but the wild horse runners gave them no mercy.

There were a few men throughout the years who felt a fondness and kind of kinship for the wild ones. When they realized what the mustang's ultimate end would be, these humane people rounded up the best specimens and worked to preserve the breed. Probably the best known benefactor is Bob Brislawn of Wyoming, who spent the last fifty years gathering up the remnants of a brave little breed. His hunt was long and difficult, because by the turn of the century most mustangs were so adulterated by domestic blood that they scarcely resembled the original mustang at all. In 1957, he helped to form the Spanish Mustang Registry, Inc. to record the animals whom he felt had pure lineage. The object of the registry is not to improve the breed but to preserve it as it was. Some of the pedigrees now go back seventy years. Several other registries are collecting stock in an attempt to create an improved mustang, but genuine mustang stock is now so limited that none of the registries are very large; the Spanish Mustang Registry has only about one hundred and twenty registered animals.

The future of the mustang, in a small way, is assured by these associations, but nothing can replace the sight of a wild band of mustangs streaming over the lip of a mesa and stretching out at a dead run on the flat plain; or a wild foal, barely dry from birth, gamely keeping up with the galloping herd; or a group of mares casually watching a violent struggle for mastery between their old stallion and an upstart intruding stallion.

Efforts have been made to establish wild horse refuges in the western states, and their success seems quite likely. Perhaps someday the wild horse will run its range again, unbranded and unbridled. Its enemies will once more be the cougar and the winter snows, but the battle will at least be a fair one.

Paso Fino

Outstanding points of conformation:

HEIGHT: average 14 hands.
COLORS AND MARKINGS: all colors, including albino and pinto. White markings allowed.
HEAD: small in proportion to body, somewhat resembles Morgan head.
NECK: long and full, well arched.
LEGS: thin with well-defined tendons.
MANE AND TAIL: exceptionally long and full; tail often brushes ground, and forelock falls more than halfway down the face. Mane and tail are left naturally long.

THERE IS an old-new breed making its presence felt in the United States. Of the same original stock as the wild mustang, this little horse called the Paso Fino (meaning "fine step" in Spanish) has fine-stepped its way into the hearts of many new American horsemen.

The most unique features about the Paso Fino horse (a true horse although it only averages 14 hands in height, for there is no pony blood in its ancestry) are its various natural gaits, the most popular of which is the *paso fino*. It is a broken pace in which the hind hoof strikes the ground a fraction of a second before the front hoof on the same side. The result is an even one, two, three, four beat, and the ride is perfectly smooth, with no rise and fall of the horse's top-line. When performing in competition, the horse is penalized if a perfect beat is not maintained.

Other gaits performed by the Paso Fino are the *paso corto* (the

speed of a fast walk, but with the same sequence as the *paso fino*, which is performed at about the speed of a slow walk), *paso largo* (the broken pace performed about as fast as a canter or fast trot), and the *andadura* (a true pace done at full speed). It also canters, this being the only gait it performs without a poised, collected manner. Interestingly enough, the Paso Fino never, ever trots; the foals *paso* from birth, often preferring the *paso corto* to an ordinary walk, for the gaits are all natural and never require training.

In addition to its captivating gaits, the Paso Fino has engaging looks and style inherited from its Andalusian, Barb, and Spanish Jennet ancestors. When Cortez had such phenomenal luck in subduing the Aztecs, it was mainly attributable to the horses that were being bred on royal breeding farms on the islands of the Caribbean by the edict of the Queen of Spain. Horses arrived in Puerto Rico in 1509, finding it to be a lumpy island, with canyons and rocky trails, hills and steep valleys. In time, the people learned that it did no good to have a fast horse, for it could go nowhere at a pace faster than a trot, anyway; since much of the breeding stock derived from the Spanish Jennet, a horse prized for its ambling or pacing gait, they began to breed for this gait and for style. For nearly two hundred years the isolation of the small island prevented the introduction of any new breeds. The inhabitants accomplished their aim — that of producing an ambling horse — but in the process of inbreeding, the horse had become even smaller than its original 14:2 hand average, so wealthy horsemen from the sugar plantations imported larger breeds to increase the size. Arabian, American Saddle Horse, Tennessee Walking Horse, and Morgan were introduced, but the Morgan was the only one that nicked (crossed) favorably. Crosses to the Arabian produced offspring without the *paso* gaits, Tennessee Walker crosses were generally gelded as plantation workhorses, and the American Saddle Horse produced no stock deemed suitable for breeding. These infusions were made prior to the Spanish-American War, and by now the Paso Fino breed is once more stabilized, the Morgan breeding being most evident in the lines of the head, although a few have the Andalusian's roman nose.

In 1943, Puerto Rico began to recognize that it had a potentially excellent breed, so it formed an association called Federación del Deporte de Caballos de silla de Puerto Rico to improve it. Before this time, no stallions had been gelded, the mares were ignored, and most breeding was indiscriminate. After the foundation of the association, quality increased rapidly; and the horse seen today is a close-coupled, graceful horse that performs all its gaits naturally with a curved neck, arched tail, and eager, forward-pointed ears. So calm are even the top show stallions that tiny children can ride them safely.

All of the usual horse colors are found among Paso Finos, including dominant white (albino) and pinto, but there are no Appaloosa markings. The variety of colors is thought to have come from the Tennessee Walker, for the more ancient bloodlines showed only bay, black, and chestnut coloring. All of the best breeding lines may be found in the United States, and the Paso

Finos are beginning to appear in horse shows. American rules insist upon naturalness, no artificial devices for showing being allowed, and the horse is always shown barefoot.

Outside the show ring, the Paso Fino is a perfect pleasure horse with few faults. Its owners use it for all manner of sports, including trail rides, mounted drills, western competition, and just plain comfortable enjoyment.

Peruvian Paso

Outstanding points of conformation:

HEIGHT: 15:1 hands or under.
COLORS AND MARKINGS: all colors, white markings common.
FACE: flat and broad.
MUZZLE: fine and neat.
JAW: clean-cut and neat.
NECK: arched and muscular.
PASTERNS: medium and strong.
LEGS: long and clean, very light and strong, one-inch diameter often seen.
HOOVES: strong, small.
HIND-QUARTERS: rather heavy, well muscled.
MANE AND TAIL: hair long and fine, left in its natural state.

FEW HORSES are more fascinating to watch in action than the Peruvian Paso. Related to the Paso Fino (both having descended from horses bred on the Caribbean Islands for use by the Conquistadores), they have evolved to different ends, for the Peruvian Paso is a larger horse, having a great deal of stamina from living in the high Andes, and with a strange sort of gait at which the front legs show a winging or "termino" action while the hind legs move along sedately behind.

The Peruvian Paso breed doesn't have any particular conformation. When standing still, it looks like nothing more than an ordinary cow pony. What gives the horse style and what makes the breed worthy of note are the great variety of gaits and way of going, as well as one of the most comfortable rides possible. Its past history is as interesting as its present.

Taken to Peru as war-horses, the Barb-Andalusians of the Spaniards were soon being bred for the most comfortable and useful gaits, and for stamina to help colonize the new land. The horses were sometimes shod with silver shoes, for there was no iron to be had; but usually they were not shod at all, for they had begun to show a peculiar and comfortable gait that included lifting the front legs very high and rolling them to the side as much as six inches at the top of the stride. Shoeing would have placed too great a weight on the tendons and muscles. In other breeds, a very similar practice of throwing the feet to the side is called "winging" and is highly condemned, but that movement is generally stiff and faulty, whereas the Peruvian Paso's rolling action comes from its loose, flexible shoulder, and actually helps it to retain good footing and balance. To watch this horse in full swing is an awe-inspiring sight, for its neck and tail are arched to the point of haughtiness and its paddling movements make it seem about to fly. As a matter of fact, it does reach speeds of up to eighteen miles per hour at this gait, and sustained speeds of eleven miles per hour. The Peruvian Paso has four other natural gaits besides the lateral-gait paso (in which the front foot is lifted before and lowered to the ground after the hind leg on that same side): the flat-footed walk, trot, canter, and running *paso* (which is a true pace performed very swiftly, the same as the Paso Fino's *andadura*). These lateral gaits make smooth riding because the horse has an odd four- to six-inch-long cartilage-like connection where the lumbar connects with the backbone, and this takes up nearly all the shock. In addition, the rolling motion of the front legs absorbs any excessive movement. Peruvian Paso owners like to describe contests in which riders on Peruvian Pasos carry full glasses of water in a race at the *paso* gait, spilling scarcely a drop along the way. The canter, although a natural gait, is usually avoided in Peru, and the trot is never performed under saddle.

The Peruvian Paso has acquired some excellent characteristics from living in the rare atmosphere of the Andes. Its lungs and heart are unusually large, giving it great capacity for deep breathing and excellent circulation. As a result, it is nearly unapproachable in stamina, its only close competitor in endurance being the Arabian. The isolation of its homeland has caused the breed traits to become very fixed, and the mares are sometimes bred to donkeys invariably producing mules with a *paso* gait. The Peruvian Paso is used continually for inspecting crops, as a means of transportation, and for carrying supplies on and between ranches. It is sometimes asked to travel as far as thirty to forty miles in a day at the *paso* gait, averaging nine miles per hour or better.

The first Peruvian Pasos to come to the United States were imported to Arizona in 1965, and by late 1967 there were more than a hundred mares, stallions, and geldings. Apparently, the Peruvian government began to have fears that the United States market would take the country's best breeding stock, so they placed a moratorium on exportation of good Peruvian mares and stallions for the next fifteen years. Presumably, this ruins any importing plans that American breeders might have had until 1981. But there are sufficient horses to form a strong foundation here, and numbers are increasing steadily. Some breeders are experimenting with crossbreeding, using Shetland, Quarter Horse, Tennessee Walking Horse, and American Saddle Horse animals. The usual result (according to reports) is a strong tendency for the offspring to have the *paso* gait.

The Peruvian Paso is a horse for all occasions. Its elegant action makes it equal to the finest parade, yet it doesn't look out of place carrying a pack or pulling a cart. It is sometimes used as a jumper and endurance horse, and its good manners make it suitable for children to ride. Although the Peruvian Paso has great stamina, it tires in time, just like any horse; but its indomitable spirit will not allow it to fall into an easier action or carriage, and it continues swiftly and elegantly on, a beautiful horse with exquisite action — a joy to ride and to own.

Pinto and Paint

Outstanding points of conformation:

HEIGHT: 12 to 17 hands.

COLORS AND MARKINGS: there are two patterns found in pinto markings, and any number of ways the two might be combined. The two definite types are as follows:

Tobiano pattern: a clean-cut pattern with large, sharply delineated borders, seldom roan. Head markings normal; usually four white stockings. Mane and tail hair the color of skin at its source. Usually a dark spot on each flank. White suspenders often present — a white strip running from front stockings up and over withers. White dominates dorsal or back region, dark covers more of the ventral or belly region. There may be a large dark spot or "shield" on chest and front of neck. Horse usually has brown eyes.

Overo pattern: Dark spots often roan with ragged edges. White markings often small and irregular. Apron of white on face common, and often whole head is white except for black ears. Mane and tail often contain roan hairs over both light and dark base areas. Legs are sometimes solidly dark, or if white, spotted with color. Suspenders seldom present; shield sometimes seen. Dorsal or back area generally dark with white abdomen, or both top and underline may be dark, and the sides white. Blue or white eyes common.

GENERAL CONFORMATION: the Paint Horse always has stock horse build, the Pinto Horse may be stock, light horse, or pony.

MANE AND TAIL: in whatever style the horse requires.

FOR YEARS, the pinto was the underdog of the horse world. Nobody wanted it. It was and still is rejected by nearly all major registries because it is spotted (although just why spots are bad

is debatable). The pinto markings were a natural part of the western horse's heritage, for some of the horses brought to the Americas by Cortez, De Soto, and later importers were pintos, which handed their markings down through the generations to the mustang of the West, that played quite a large role in the development of the Quarter Horse. Why the American Quarter Horse Association chose to bar spotted horses with excellent bloodlines from its registry has always puzzled the pinto admirer. That rejection, plus the refusal of other registries to tolerate the pinto's presence, relegated the pinto to the back pasture, destined to be the farm pet and unlettered utility and ranch horse.

In the days of the early West, the pinto was not discriminated against. In fact, its splashy coloring made it worth at least fifty dollars more than a solid-colored horse of the same ability and quality. And in those days, it acquired a wealth of descriptive names. Spotted ponies in Britain and the eastern United States had always been called skewbald if brown-and-white, and piebald if black-and-white. The cowboys apparently paid little attention to these ready-made names, and manufactured their own. Some of them, all applying equally to either color combination, were calico, paint, pinto, patch, and Indian pony. The names tobiano and overo were applied to certain types and patterns of spots. Many times pintos were sold by unscrupulous dealers as Arabian horses (a ruse which brought exhorbitant prices for a good many ordinary pinto ponies). Many pintos have blue or white eyes. The westerners called them china-eyes, glass-eyes, walleyes, cotton-eyes, and blue-eyes. The horse with just one

light eye is sometimes called watch-eyed. Such light-pigmented eyes are not defective.

The Appaloosa seems to be a type of pinto, but since its spots sometimes do not appear until it is several months old, it is felt in some quarters that the Appaloosa is not a true pinto. An ordinary pinto's markings are always present at birth.

Two registries are now in existence for the promotion of the pinto horse. One registry, the Pinto Horse Association, registers any pinto horse with good conformation in whatever breed type it happens to fall. Many pintos registered with this association are three- and five-gaited horses, jumpers, racers, and pleasure horses. It also registers ponies as small as 12 hands. This registry looks after the average pinto and encourages the upbreeding of all by awarding outstanding breeders special places in the Stud Book. The other registry is the American Paint Horse Association, and its goal is to create a specific breed-type of spotted horses with Quarter Horse or Thoroughbred breeding. In order to be eligible for registry, a prospective Paint Horse must be sired by either a registered Quarter Horse, a Thoroughbred, or another Paint Horse. It must be at least 14 hands, and may not be a gaited horse (a term applied by this association to include horses that single-foot or pace, but not to those that fox-trot or do the running walk).

The terms paint and pinto have caused some confusion. Originally, the terms did not designate stock horses versus gaited or non-stock type horses. They referred to a type of spot pattern, overo being paint, and tobiano being pinto, both of which are described at the beginning of the pinto section. Most western horses were tobianos, so the word pinto came also to mean any spotted horse.

The Indians were fond of their brightly splashed ponies. They enjoyed cutting a dashing figure, and were so entranced with the spots that they often dabbled around with pigments and added their own designs to the pattern. They used hand-prints, and rings around the horses's eyes, and various symbolic markings for good luck in hunting or war.

Of course, all pinto markings didn't come from the mustangs. They are found in many other breeds on occasion (the Icelandic Pony, for instance, without a trace of mustang breeding), and it is said that a cross of hot- and cold-blooded horses sometimes produces pintos. The occasional pinto that appears in well-established breeds which have abolished pintos is considered a black sheep and an embarrassment. Minor markings that will condemn an otherwise fine horse are white markings on the upper legs or body, and markings outside the rectangle of the face formed by the ears, eyes, and nostrils. Perhaps it should be noted at this point that many Arabians have small white markings on their underlines.

It is shameful that the pinto has been maligned all these years. Perhaps it is because a brightly colored pinto which gives a bad performance is remembered long after a bad solid-color horse is forgotten. Fortunately for this smartly painted horse, the public has finally come to its defense and has led it out of that lonely back pasture to rejoin the colorful world of pedigreed horses.

The Quarter Horse is the horse of the West. Many of its forebears were of mustang stock caught wild on the prairies and taken into the remudas. The original stock is probably that of the Chickasaw Horses, which were captured from De Soto's herd by the Chickasaw Indians of Carolina, Virginia, and Tennessee. The Chickasaw Horse was a short-bodied pony-size horse with a great deal of stamina and speed. It still exists today in its original form, but its major offshoot, the Quarter Horse, was the result of crossing the little Chickasaw with the colonists' horses. The horses of that time (in the 1600's) were chiefly of English stock brought by the first colonists (early colonists of Jamestown, Virginia, had to import horses twice because they ate the first bunch). The first English racing horses were imported to Virginia about 1620, and Governor Nicholson of Virginia conveniently legalized horse racing shortly thereafter. By 1690, enthusiasm had grown so great that large purses were being offered for the match races, which were races in which two horses ran a quarter of a mile, usually along Main Street (since there was seldom any other place straight and long enough to run a race), the winner taking the prize. The winners of these short races weren't the pure Thoroughbreds, but the Thoroughbred-Chickasaw crosses, and this was the beginning of the Quarter Horse — the horse that could run a quarter of a mile faster than any other horse of those times. Some of the better known Thoroughbreds used for crossbreeding purposes were Imported Janus, Imp. Sir Archy, and others.

When the settlers started to move west, their horses went with them, and along the way picked up such breeding as Arabian, Morgan, Standardbred, and various miscellaneous blood. The Quarter Horse type got quite a bit of impetus from such horses as Steeldust and Copperbottom in Texas. The Steeldust blood was so prepotent that for many years all horses of the Quarter Horse type were known as Steeldust horses. The stock horse went by the name of Steeldust until the AQHA was formed in 1941, changing the name to Quarter Horse. The name "quarter horse" had, up until that time, designated horses that could run a quarter of a mile with good speed, and many sprinting Thoroughbreds were called quarter horses even though they had pure Thoroughbred lineage. Most Quarter Horses of today can be traced to the great Peter McCue, which was foaled in 1895, and a high percentage have a large portion of recent Thoroughbred blood. Almost all of the sires in Volume I of the American Quarter Horse Stud Book had at least 50 percent Thoroughbred breeding.

The Quarter Horse is an unexcelled sprinter. Even the swift Thoroughbred cannot outrun the Quarter Horse for distances of up to 440 yards, or about a quarter of a mile. At major racing tracks in the United States, the Quarter Horses vie with one another for some of the highest purses in racing history, including Thoroughbred purses. But speed isn't everything, and the Quarter Horse, for all its variation in conformation, type, and style, is one of the most versatile horses in the world. As a quarter-mile racer it is unbeaten. As a jumper and hunter, it is beginning to find a place in this wide-open field, and classes for jumping have been added to regular AQHA horse shows as performance events. The Quarter Horse is a perfectly adapted trail and endurance horse, and its calm disposition gets it over obstacles that would discourage any other horse. For barrel racing and gymkhana events, no other horse can outdo the speedy Quarter Horse, and it is game for making impossibly fast spins around the barrels or poles. No other horse can take its place in utility ranch work, and it is so fast on its feet that it has even come into favor as a polo pony. A good Quarter Horse is often a better polo pony than the more commonly used Thoroughbred, for it is stronger and closer to ground, it is accomplished at turning on a dime, and it has a level-headed calmness necessary for such a rough sport. In comparison to the Thoroughbred, the Quarter Horse often has shorter legs, more powerfully muscled quarters, and it carries its head lower as a rule. Whether or not a low-slung head is a good point in a polo pony is debatable, but it is quite suitable for the stock horse, for if the head and neck are well out in front rather than high and up, the horse is easier to neck-rein and its head doesn't get in the way of the rope or the rider's vision. In addition, the horse can better see what is going on around its feet, and this is invaluable for trail riding when the horse must watch what it is doing or it will get itself and its rider into all kinds of unfortunate situations.

Ranch work is what the Quarter Horse was designed for, with perhaps an occasional race thrown in for excitement. Through the years, the Quarter Horse has come to have a kind of sixth sense about what a cow plans to do next, and since it knows what the cow will do, it knows what to do to foil the cow. Perhaps one of the most exciting classes at a horse show is the cutting class, wherein a horse and rider must cut or separate a calf from a herd of other calves and take it to the other side of the arena. This sounds as if it would be fairly simple until the conditions of the game are examined, and one finds out that the horse is to do all the thinking and action after it is shown which calf is wanted by the rider. Otherwise, the rider is just there for looks, riding with a loose rein and no aids, and the horse must be smart and quick enough to cut out the specified calf then take it where it is to go. And a frightened, obstinate calf is very reluctant to leave the protection of the herd. Some cutting horses even use their teeth to good advantage.

This, then, is the Quarter Horse: quick and willing and above all, intelligent; able to stop and start again and again without complaint; calm in the face of the unexpected; patient with even an unsure rider; sure-footed on the trail; and able to carry heavy weight for a long time. It is easy to see why the Quarter Horse has found favor, and a fairly good bet to say that it will probably remain a favorite for many years to come.

Rangerbred

Outstanding points of conformation:

HEIGHT: 15:3 to 16:2 hands.

COLORS AND MARKINGS: the Rangerbred is one of the most vividly and variously marked of the horse breeds. As well as the normal solid, pinto, and albino coloring, the Rangerbred sports Appaloosa patterns and an incredible combination of those patterns, plus pinto, plus all sorts of roans, duns, and dapples. White markings are common.

GENERAL CONFORMATION: stock horse conformation, no special points.

MANE AND TAIL: especially on the Appaloosa-marked horses, the mane and tail are full and flowing, which differentiates them from the Appaloosa Horse. Both are trimmed western style.

IT IS General Grant, former President of the United States, who must be credited with the responsibility of forming the beginnings of the Colorado Rangerbred Horse. After his two terms of presidency were finished, Grant decided, in 1878, to take a world tour. Arriving in Turkey, he was warmly greeted by the Sultan, who honored him with a gift of two stallions, a Barb which Grant named Linden Tree, and an Arabian he called Leopard. A friend of General Grant's, General Colby, who had a cattle ranch in Beatrice, Nebraska, persuaded Grant to loan him Linden Tree and Leopard for the breeding season of 1894, and in this short time the two oriental stallions sired a multitude of foals out of range mares. The foals were striking animals having great presence combined with

native intelligence, and word of them spread around the country until it reached a group of ranchers in Kit Carson County, Colorado. They were greatly impressed with the rumors and sent an emissary out to see if it were all true. He was impressed, too, as everyone else who had seen them was, and he returned with a black-eared white stallion named Tony, a double grandson of Leopard, and a herd of promising mares of both Linden Tree and Leopard breeding. This was the nucleus of the Colorado Rangerbred, a horse reknowned for its cow savvy and horse sense, its abilities as a utility horse, and particularly its odd assortment of colors.

Another addition of Barb blood was made by the new owners in 1918, with the use of an Algiers stallion known as Spotte. Some Standardbred blood was also infused, and the herd was inbred and line-bred to produce a definite breed.

The Rangerbred people insist that they don't breed for color, but it would be safe to wager that were they to choose between two horses of equal ability, the horse with the more bizarre coloring would come out ahead. And some of the colors and patterns are odd, indeed. All of the usual Appaloosa patterns are represented, and some of the Rangerbreds are double-registered with the Appaloosa Horse Club (this is not a reciprocal registration, for registered Appaloosas may not be registered in the Rangerbred registry unless both parents are Rangerbreds with proper pedigrees).

The splashly markings are considered by the breeders to have come down through the Barb side of the pedigree, but it is also possible that the native mares had some Appaloosa blood in them, for by that time the spotted horses of the Nez Percé Indians had been well scattered throughout the West and Midwest.

It has been stated by some authorities that crossing the pure Arab or Barb upon horses of cold-blooded, northern European, and Asian extract will produce a wealth of off-colors and pintos. One possible example was The Tetrarch, an English Thoroughbred of undefeated racing fame in the second decade of this century. The Tetrarch, known popularly as The Spotted Wonder, was a gray horse with typical Appaloosa markings in the form of squaw marks (round or oval spots) over his entire body. He passed this colorful coat down in modified form to a chestnut with white spatterings, known in recent years to the American public and racing circles as Candy Spots.

But the Rangerbred coloring is not confined to Appaloosa markings, although these seem to prevail. There are all the standard colors, from bay and sorrel to blacks. There are blue, gray, and mauve grullas with black points, smoky duns and bright orange claybank duns, roans with sabino (sorrel) spots, flea-bitten roans, strawberry, blue, and red-speckled roans, dappled grays that whiten with age, and overo and tobiano pintos. They interbreed and are intentionally crossed so randomly (color isn't considered, while utility and conformation are) that some very interesting combinations occur as well as some nearly indescribable colors and combinations of patterns.

The Colorado Rangerbred Horse Association, Inc., is not an open registry. That is, all registered horses must trace back to the original Barb and Arab stallions. The registry has no particular requirements or standards for conformation except that each horse be as near the ideal cow horse as possible. This is an unusual attitude, and might stem from the fact that the association adopted many of its rules from the American Jockey Club, which also has no such qualifications.

The majority of Rangerbred raising is being done in Texas, but as the Rangerbred continues to increase in numbers and popularity, it is spreading to the other western states as well, being used for all ranch work as well as being a pleasure horse of good quality.

Standardbred

Outstanding points of conformation:

HEIGHT: 15 to 16:2 hands.
COLORS AND MARKINGS: most solid colors, including bay, brown, chestnut, roan, gray, and black, in that order. White markings are rare.
HEAD: bones are prominent and nicely formed.
FACE: profile is straight, flat across the eyes, although roman nose is sometimes seen.
NECK: usually straight without much if any crest, medium length and not thick or thin.
WITHERS: are sometimes lower than the croup.
CROUP: on pacers is sometimes steep and short.
MANE AND TAIL: left flowing, but the tail is sometimes slightly trimmed so it doesn't get in the sulky driver's face.

THE STANDARDBRED is a remodeled Thoroughbred. The remodeling was accomplished quite some time ago (in fact, nearly half a century ago), so that the Standardbred is really a new breed by now, with different conformation, capabilities, and temperament, but the breeding has been mostly Thoroughbred from start to finish. The foundation sire of the Standardbred breed was Messenger, a gray Thoroughbred imported from England in 1788 for racing in the United States. As time went by, it was noticed that a remarkable number of his progeny had a knack for really fast trotting. His great-grandson, Rysdyck's Hambletonian, born in 1849, has been called the Father of Modern Standardbreds, and all but 1 percent of all Standardbreds trace back to him. He sired 1330 foals, with both trotting and pacing abilities, and much legend has built up around him although he was never raced himself.

Few horses other than the Thoroughbred could, at that time, trot with any speed or style. The Morgan probably came the closest, and there is a dash of Morgan blood in the Standardbred's lineage. There is a bit of other miscellaneous blood in its past, too, for during the Standardbred's early days, any horse that could trot a mile in 2:30 minutes or could pace a mile in 2:25 minutes, could be entered in the Standardbred Stud Book. Thus came the origin of the breed name, for any horse that could equal or surpass the standard set by the registry was "standard bred." The standard has been repeatedly lowered, and it now stands at 2:20 minutes.

The Standardbred is a harness racer. That is, he races at a trot or pace in harness, pulling a small vehicle, or sulky, and his driver behind him. Harness racing has been going on for quite a long time, since the very beginning of written or illustrated history. The horses pulling chariots were harness racers, and ancient scripts and sculpture from before 700 B.C. depict harnessed horses pulling small carts and their drivers.

The vehicle to be pulled by the racing horse has always posed problems. The aim has always been to make the sulky as light as possible, yet strong enough to hold up under the stiff punishment it must take during the race or the several heats of the race. Before the turn of the century, the sulky cart had high wheels and was quite heavy. It had been introduced prior to the Civil War (before that time, most trotting races were done with the riders on the horses or with heavy wagons) and lasted until 1893 when the bicycle-wheel sulky came into existence. Improvements came mostly one by one, with the wheels decreasing in size until now they are only about two feet in diameter. Aluminum now takes the place of steel parts, plastic replaces others, and there has been

a general improvement in streamlining and utility. The speed records have been bettered accordingly, for along with the changes in the sulky there have major advancements in the care and training of horses. The Standardbred of today is a much better specimen than its forerunners, having the advantage of decades of intensive and careful breeding behind it. Two-year-olds regularly reach times that the completely developed and seasoned older horses of fifty years ago could not touch. The best trotting time in 1845, for instance, was 2:29½ minutes for the mile. By 1894 the time had improved to 2:03¾ for both trotters and pacers. Stallions and mares have usually proven to be slower trotters than geldings, although the mares are generally faster than stallions. Interestingly, and perhaps coincidently, all record-setting trotting champions since 1912 have been geldings, and all pacing record makers since 1896 have been stallions. In 1938, the gelding Greyhound set the trotting record at 1:55¼. The stallion Adios Butler set a new pacing record of 1:54⅗ in 1960. Pacers are usually one to three seconds faster than trotters on the average.

The trot is more or less a diagonal gait, that is, the front and hind feet on opposite sides strike the ground nearly at the same time. Usually, the rear foot on one side will hit the ground slightly before the front foot on the opposite side, but since the interval is so small, it sound almost like one beat. The pace is very different, being what is called a lateral gait, with both right legs moving forward in unison, then both left legs. It is an interesting gait to watch, for the horse seems to sway from side to side with a rolling motion (the common slang term for pacer is "side-wheeler"). To insure that the horse doesn't "break" or switch from the pace into the trot or a gallop, most pacers wear what are called hobbles or hopples. They consist of leather straps encircling the front and hind legs on the same side to keep the legs moving together. The trotter wears a shoe weighing about eight ounces, while the pacer's shoe only weighs about five ounces. It is the shoe that determines how the horse shall go if it is able to both trot and pace, for the changing of the shoe type and weight will turn a pacer immediately into a trotter, and vice versa. Some talented horses can trot and pace equally well, but most horses do only one. There are trotting strains and pacing strains in the Standardbred breed.

As a rule, the pacer is never matched against the trotter, the two only meeting during qualifying races when the horses race against time to establish whether or not the individual can meet the track's speed standards. The Standardbred usually races at speeds of twenty-five to thirty miles per hour for a mile. The speeds when coming out of the gate and when in the homestretch sometimes approach thirty-five miles per hour. A Standardbred is estimated at averaging five lengths per second.

Most Standardbred races are limited to eight horses, because of the width of the sulkies and the dangers involved in racing if there are too many entrants on the field fighting for the best position. The handicapper tries to match horses with equal capabilities, and accomplishes part of his handicapping by the relative position he gives to each horse in regard to the rail. The spot nearest the rail is the most favorable place because the distance is slightly shorter, and this is the position that all drivers will jockey for. At fairs and on the Grand Circuit sulky racing tracks, races are usually run in heats (a heat is one race of a series). If pari-mutuel betting is involved, only one dash determines the winner. The usual length of the track is a mile or a half-mile, but tracks of three-fourths and five-eighths miles are becoming more popular now.

The Standardbred has a great deal of endurance, which enables it to go out and run a race, then after a short rest period, to go out and run it again. The old-time racing during the last century was even more grueling than it is today, for the distances run and the weight of the sulkies were much greater. In those days, a race might consist of five heats in which the winner was the horse with the three best times out of the five races. Some of the most popular present-day races are the regularly scheduled night races. Betting is usually quite high, and heats are seldom run, the winner being announced after each race or dash. No horse is allowed to compete for money after it passes its fifteenth year.

Some of the more popular harness racers bring excellent prices at auction, although they don't begin to bring the prices paid for Thoroughbreds. Adios Butler, the record-making pacer, was sold to a syndicate in 1960 for $600,000. His sire Adios was sold for $500,000 in 1954, and is reknowned for standing at stud for the highest fee paid for any breed at that time — a whopping $15,000.

When racing, a harness horse uses a very long stride with little folding at the knees or hocks, and its feet skim just above the surface of the ground. Its head is held high by the use of a checkrein running from the bit, over the top of the head, and back to a hook on the harness. The reason for the checkrein and the high head carriage is that the horse maintains a more even gait and longer stride with its head up, and is easier to control. The raising is done gradually over the nine-month schooling period that precedes the horse's appearance on the track, so that it is quite accustomed to it by the time it begins to race.

A Standardbred has the general points of the Thoroughbred except that it is more angular, heavier, and closer to the ground. Its legs are usually placed well back to give added push and longer stride, and it often has a steeper croup than is seen on the Thoroughbred. It is not highly regarded as a riding horse, because a trotting horse is not as comfortable to ride as a horse that walks or gallops, but it often gets a good hunter if crossed on the Thoroughbred. Such crosses were once utilized by the United States Cavalry, and the Standardbred was enthusiastically used as a range stud in the Old West for the fine road and harness horses it produced.

Tennessee Walking Horse

Outstanding points of conformation:

HEIGHT: average 15:2.

COLORS AND MARKINGS: sorrels, chestnuts, blacks, roans, whites, bays, browns, grays, duns. Pintos are grudgingly admitted. White markings often extensive.

FACE: is usually roman-nosed but not always.

EYES: white of eye frequently is shown.

NECK: muscular and well developed.

PASTERNS: long and sloping well.

BODY: ribs well sprung, and underline well let down at flank.

HOCK: tendency toward sickle hock (a common fault in which the hock is "bent" so that the cannon bone doesn't stand perpendicular to the ground, but points forward).

MANE AND TAIL: are left full and long, the tail is set.

FEW THINGS are more exciting to see than a Tennessee Walking Horse swinging into a ground-eating running walk or a rocking, springy canter. The canter is often overlooked by those who describe the breed because the running walk is such an extraordinary achievement, but it well deserves a word of mention. At a collected canter, the Tennessee Walker more resembles a child's rocking horse than anything else. Its movements are fluid and without jolt, and the up and down action is exaggerated, like a ball bobbing in a pond. The running walk, which has made the breed famous, is a greatly extended flat walk with an overstep of as much as twelve to fifty inches (the overstep is the distance the hind foot oversteps

the track just made by the front foot). Too much overstep will cause an unbalanced gait and an unpleasant ride.

Photos made of performing Tennessee Walkers always show them at the highest point of the stride, with the front leg raised to its peak and a maximum distance between the two hind legs. To make the horse seem to have more power and lifting action, nearly all photographs are arranged so that the ground the horse is traveling over seems to rise at a sharp slope, incorrectly showing the horse going uphill. Such pictures should be viewed at the opposite slant if the true picture is desired.

The running walk is performed at speeds between twelve and sixteen miles per hour among show animals, although the greater speeds are often deplored by proponents of the breed because they do not demonstrate the speed that the Tennessee Walking Horse was bred for — a gait of between six and eight miles per hour, designed to get the rider somewhere fast in a comfortable manner with neither horse nor rider tired on arrival. The ride is very comfortable, being almost a glide, and the head nods to take up much of the normal jolt usually encountered in the walk. When the head is at its lowest point, the ears flop sideways and down, and sometimes the teeth click. Gaits required of the Tennessee Walker are the walk, running walk, and the canter.

The Tennessee Walking Horse has been bred for about a hundred years, stemming from a melting pot of breeds brought to Tennessee plantations. The first progenitors were native mares and Thorough-

bred stallions. The good riding horses obtained from this match were crossed in later years with Standardbred, Morgan, American Saddle Horse, Narragansett, and Canadian Pacing Horses to produce a comfortable, well-gaited, all-around utility horse. They were referred to as Plantation Walkers, "turn-rows," and "nodders," and euphemistically, as "Nature's Rocking Chair." The running walk gait was carefully selected and cultivated from among the odd gaits turned up by the mixed breeding. One of the major early breeders was the great horse Copperbottom, of Quarter Horse fame; and Allan F-1 (the F-1 seems to stand for Foundation Horse #1). The latter, of Standardbred, Narragansett, and Morgan breeding, was chosen to be the foundation sire. He had great ability at the pace and trot, and a trot record of 2:25, a really excellent time for the 1890's.

The Tennessee plantation owners were conscientious horse breeders, and even though there was no breed association or stud book until 1935, records were kept meticulously and little information was lost. The owner's or breeder's name was often combined with the horse's name, such as Brantley's Roan Allen, Jr., Ramsey's Rena, etc., thus providing a kind of oral lineage.

Today, the tendency to do the running walk is inherited, and many Walkers fall into it naturally, although all need training to perfect it to show quality. Shoes are not necessary for its execution, but sometimes a keg shoe is worn, and pads on the front feet create more action. Most Tennessee Walking Horses are used mainly for pleasure, trail rides, stock horses, and utility horses, but the ones destined for the tanbark are put through rigorous training. Their tails are set, and they are prepared in the same manner as the American Saddle Horse. The Saddle Seat Equitation used in the ring is of the unsightly leaning-back variety, but the trend seems to be shifting to a more balanced seat.

Tennessee Walking Horses have been gaining steadily in popularity, especially in the South and southeastern parts of the United States, although they are also used by the Canadian Mounted Police and western forest rangers. This is a horse on its way up, ridden by 4-H'ers, cattlemen, hunters, and housewives alike, all with a contagious enthusiasm that is impossible to ignore.

Thoroughbred

Outstanding points of conformation:

HEIGHT: 15:3 to 17 hands. Body is streamlined, muscles very flat.
COLORS AND MARKINGS: usually solid, bay, chestnut, black, brown. Gray occasionally found, but no albinos, palominos, or pintos. White markings frequently seen.
HEAD: wide between the eyes, straight or dished profile.
UNDERLINE: is usually drawn up when horse is in racing condition.
HIP: length from hip to hock is very great.
GASKIN: is flat and long, not crescent.
MANE AND TAIL: thin and fine; mane is usually shortened by pulling to about four inches, and tail falls a little below hock.

MORE HAS BEEN written about the Thoroughbred than about any other breed of horses. Racing results appear daily in major newspapers, giving speeds and times and any other information that might have been dredged up about the favorites. A racer's pulled tendons are reported and mourned with as much or more sincerity than a popular public figure's might be. Every Thoroughbred racer's genealogy is a matter of public record, and is memorized and calculated upon by every racing enthusiast with a racing form. And people who have never seen a horse race eagerly grab up turf news to see if their favorite was in the winnings for the latest race.

Many racing buffs know less than nothing about the Thoroughbred as a horse, but could tell its history and speed records with fair accuracy, beginning in England with the importations of the saddle horse Byerly Turk in 1689, the Darley Arabian from Syria in 1706, and the Godolphin Barb, foaled in Barbary in 1724. These three eastern sires formed the foundation of the entire Thoroughbred breed, most of the credit going to the Darley Arabian

through Eclipse, his great-great-grandson. Most importing to England of oriental horses (174 of them in all) was done before 1750. By this time, the English Thoroughbred was so well developed that it could make better time than the imported horses, so it might be said that the breed was established by 1750.

Most importing of Thoroughbreds to America was done between 1730 and 1800. They first appeared in Virginia and Carolina, and both George Washington and Thomas Jefferson were proud owners of hot-blooded horses. The date generally marking the beginning of Thoroughbred breeding and racing in America is 1745.

At this time, all jockeys used the method of sitting tall and leaning back in the saddle with long stirrups, thus placing most of the load on the weakest point of the horse's back. This style persisted until the jockey Tod Sloan, in 1909, managed to revolutionize the inefficient riding method by introducing the monkey crouch, with short stirrups and with the jockey in a doubled-up position over the horse's neck and shoulders. This put the jockey's weight where the horse could carry it more easily, and speed times improved accordingly.

The most famous and certainly the most popular racing horse in American history was Man o' War, often fondly referred to as Big Red. He was a tremendous horse with extraordinary ability to run, winning races by as much as one hundred lengths (a length being the average length of a horse) under cruelly heavy weights, and with odds of one hundred to one against him. Man o' War was raced only as a two- and three-year-old in 1919 and 1920, racing twenty-one times and only losing one, placing second, due to poor riding by his jockey (he later beat the winner of that race in a decisive victory). He set a world's record for

winnings at that time, only a few dollars short of a quarter of a million, and when he was retired it was with honor, being used very sparingly as a stud (his owner Sam Riddle only permitted him to serve twenty-five mares per year, and many of them were from his own stables) until he died in 1947 at the age of thirty. The public flocked to see Big Red when he was alive, and still they come to see his grave — a living epitaph for a great horse.

The making of a race horse is a complicated thing. Its parents are chosen with infinite care, and even before it is born it is entered in at least one futurity. Those that fail to live up to expectations often end up as polo ponies, hunters, and jumpers, and sometimes as studs for upgrading other breeds and types. Occasionally, for one reason or another, young horses go to auction and are sometimes bought for incredibly high prices by speculators. A price record set in 1968 for a yearling was $405,000. Some stallions are astronomically priced, and to buy them there has come into being a thing called syndication, a sort of group ownership, with the original owner keeping a large interest in the horse while selling "shares" to other people. Any winnings and/or stud fees (the stud fees are sometimes as high as two thousand dollars) are split among the group according to the size of each member's share. Some horses have been syndicated for as much as $2,500,000. This is not as expensive as it sounds, since Thoroughbreds have been exceeding $1,000,000 in track winnings for a long time, Citation being the first millionaire Thoroughbred.

Many horses are ridden before they are two years old, and all start training at the age of one. A Thoroughbred may be born any time of the year, but it is considered to be one year old the following January. Therefore, most mares are scheduled to foal as early as possible in the spring. Thoroughbreds in the Southern Hemisphere have a head start on those born in the north, for their spring arrives six months earlier.

One inescapable facet of racing is handicapping. The better and faster a horse can run, the more heavily it will be handicapped, thus giving all horses an equal chance to win a given race. Handicapping is accomplished by adding dead weight to the racer's load. The amount of weight is calculated with numerous points in mind: the horse's previous racing record, health, condition of the track, the jockey, the sex of the horse, ability to carry weight, disposition, and any shipping it might have recently experienced. These variables make the assignment of racing weights a real science calling for a sharp mind. Handicapping does make it a fair race for the least able horses, but it seems a bit unfair that the finest and fastest horses must suffer such loads. Dead weight is heavier to carry than live weight, since it doesn't accommodate itself to the movement of the horse like a jockey does.

Most tracks in the United States are one mile to one and a quarter miles long, and a recent world record for the mile was set by a horse named Buckpasser, in 1966, which won the Arlington Classic in Chicago at a speed of 1:32⅗. This was on a dirt track, as most American courses are, but the trend is switching to grass tracks like the Santa Anita track in California. Nearly all overseas racing is done on grass, for it is easier on the horse and rider. Unfortunately, the grass hinders the horse and gives slower speeds.

The Thoroughbred's life is a hard life. It starts its training and often even ends its racing career before it has completely reached maturity. The legs take a terribly hard beating in racing, and many Thoroughbreds are "buck-kneed," or over at the knees, for the strain weakens the immature ligaments which brace up the joint. A racing horse resembles a greyhound with its slim lines and tucked-up belly. When the horse is in good racing form, it may weigh only a thousand pounds, but when turned out to pasture, it may put on as much as four hundred pounds more, giving it a completely different appearance. If raced while in pasture condition, its speed would be considerably slower because of all the extra weight.

A reputation for nervous temperament has attached itself to the Thoroughbred, and in many cases this is true. As with any breeding program, close breeding does create a high-strung animal. Part of the nervousness is a result of intensive training, and a Thoroughbred often calms down considerably when retired from the track. Those that have been used in other fields, such as riding, hunting, or jumping, may never be especially nervous at all.

The Thoroughbred is bred to run. Its walk is usually lacking in polish, and its trot is often uncomfortable. There are notable exceptions, but as a general rule it makes a poor riding horse. As a hunter and jumper, however, it really shines. The difference between the hunter and jumper is that the hunter is a field horse and an economical jumper, while the jumper is a show horse trained for high, clean jumping in competition. The United States Olympic Team uses Thoroughbreds exclusively. A good jumper often has different characteristics from a racer. It stands a little taller, and many are slightly goose-rumped (sloping croup) for better footing when jumping. Besides jumping and racing, the Thoroughbred is used extensively in the crossbreeding business.

Its crossbreeding reputation began when it was first introduced to this country and used to upgrade the local mares of colonial America. In time, it was used to help form the Morgan, American Saddle Horse, Standardbred, and Quarter Horse breeds.

But the Thoroughbred really found its place in the breeding field through the efforts of the Remount Service. The Remount Service was a government stud service, under which the government provided mostly Thoroughbred (also a few Morgan, Standardbred, and Arabian) sires to be used on privately owned grade animals, then offered excellent prices for the offspring. Thus the government was assured a good supply of cavalry, field, and officers' horses, while the farmer profited by having good sires for his grade mares. After World War II there was no need for cavalry, and the Remount Service ceased operation. The last army cavalry horse was buried June 1, 1968, at Fort Riley, Kansas. The Remount heartily promoted the registering of half-breds and there is now a strong private movement behind half-bred production and popularity. Most racing Quarter Horses are half-Thoroughbred, as are racing Appaloosas. Hunters are often half-breds, the Welsh-Thoroughbred being a popular small hunter.

Few other breeds have the Thoroughbred's spirit. Many great hunters, jumpers, and racers have hobbled stubbornly to the finish line with pulled tendons or broken legs, after accidents that would have finished a horse without the grand qualities of heart and courage of the American Thoroughbred.

Ponies

THE CONFORMATION OF the pony roughly follows that of the horse, except that fewer manage to reach it. It hasn't been until recent years that the pony has been anything more than a kid pony, and many of the pony breeds found in America are just newly arrived — either from some other country or from some crossing of other breeds — and haven't had time, really, to get in shape.

For the most part, though, the pony will fall under horse specifications, with the following exceptions usually noted in pony breeds:

Points of conformation:

HEIGHT: no minimum height, but the maximum height is 14:2 hands.

HEAD: is usually a little larger in respect to the pony's size than is the horse's.

NECK: except in the highly developed show ponies, most ponies have sturdy, thick necks, often somewhat crested.

SHOULDERS: often tend to be a little straighter than the ideal 45 degrees.

LEGS: are short in comparison to the size of the body. A pony will often have a horse-size body, but its short legs make it a pony.

UNDERLINE: the underline of the pony is well let down, and many ponies tend to be potty.

RIBS: are unusually well sprung, often making the pony roly-poly and hard to fit a saddle on.

CROUP: few except the very best ponies have long, straight croups: they tend to be well muscled and rounded.

MANE AND TAIL: of most ponies is thick and quite full, especially on ponies with much north European breeding.

Appaloosa Pony

Outstanding points of conformation:

HEIGHT: 10 to 13:3 hands.

COLORS AND MARKINGS: the Appaloosa Pony shows all the patterns, particolored skin, and striped hooves of the Appaloosa Horse, the only difference between the two being size.

GENERAL CONFORMATION: is that of the Appaloosa Horse.

MANE AND TAIL: are naturally sparse, and are trimmed or left untrimmed depending upon whether or not the pony is shown as a western pony, a hunter, or as a saddle pony.

THE WILDLY SPOTTED Appaloosa Ponies have a special attraction for children. Their small size, naturally, is of first interest to the child, but after that is assured, the variable markings and colorful coats add a technicolor bonus which makes the National Appaloosa Pony one of the most rapidly increasing pony breeds in America.

Like the Appaloosa Horse, no Appaloosa Pony ever has exactly the same color pattern as any other pony, and this is another factor which makes a child cherish his Appaloosa Pony — the fact that there's not another pony like it anywhere, and that it is distinctly different, unquestionably his own pony.

The Appaloosa Pony resembles the Appaloosa Horse in everything but size. Its general conformation is the same, as are the typical markings, white sclera around the eye (sometimes called a fried-egg eye), and particolored skin around the nostrils, lips, and genital area. The resemblance should not be surprising, for many of these ponies have the very same breeding as the finest Appaloosa Horses and long pedigrees in the Appaloosa Horse Club Stud Book, but because of their small size they are barred from registration in it.

There are different varieties of ponies in the National Appaloosa Pony Association (NAPA). While some have faultless Appaloosa color and breeding, others have unknown bloodlines but excellent coloring. And there are some without the Appaloosa color but with at least one National Appaloosa Pony parent. All these ponies may be registered, provided they have good conformation and are desirable for breeding, but the improperly colored ponies must be placed in a tentative position until they prove their ability to produce spotted foals (a stallion must have twelve foals registered, and a mare must have three foals registered). Lip tattooing is employed to make positive identification possible. Any pony with pinto or albino blood will be ineligible for registration.

The ponies are divided into two classes to make competiiton among them more equal. The Class A pony measures between forty and forty-eight inches, and the Class B pony measures forty-eight to fifty-five inches. A Class B pony at the top of its limit is sometimes mistaken for a small Appaloosa Horse by the casual observer.

There is another registry for spotted ponies called the Pony of the Americas Club (POA). Many ponies with Appaloosa markings are double-registered, that is, recorded in both registries. During the formative years of each registry (they are of about the same age) many ponies have been eligible for both. Differences will be found, however, in the ruling by the POA Club that ponies under forty-six inches or 11:2 hands, or over fifty-four or 13:2 hands, may not be registered as POA's. Their idea is to create a pony for the larger child, yet to provide a gap between the Pony of the Americas and the Appaloosa Horse. A more radical difference between the two organizations is that the National Appaloosa Pony Association is preserving the Appaloosa Pony as it is found, while the POA is creating a new breed. More about the POA may be found in that section.

The National Appaloosa Pony is an extremely versatile little animal. Its popularity has spread eastward in the United States, and it isn't uncommon at all to see it under English tack or in fine harness. As a matter of fact, it is more rule than exception in parts of Canada and England, where it has carved a substantial foothold.

The future is promising for the little Appaloosa Pony. Racing has become a popular event for youngsters and their ponies, and the ponies reach some excellent speeds for their size. Jumping, reining, and harness are all the domain of the Appaloosa Pony, and for fun riding it ranks among the best. As a matter of fact, adults seem to get quite as comfortable a ride on it as the children do.

Chincoteague Pony

Outstanding points of conformation:

HEIGHT: 12 to 13:2 hands. Likely to become taller in the future.
COLORS AND MARKINGS: gray, sorrel, bay, black, and pinto. White markings common.
GENERAL CONFORMATION: no particular conformation — typical pony shape now, but likely to become more refined in the near future.
MANE AND TAIL: thick and full.

THE SPRING of 1967 heralded the beginning of the end for the chubby little Chincoteague Pony made famous in book and movie. It isn't that the ponies of Assateague and Chincoteague islands, off the coast of northern Virginia, are disappearing; it is simply that they are being absorbed and changed by the blood of the spirited gray Arabian, Skowreym, who stands 14:2 hands and is descended from the famous Skowronek. Skowreym was stud for the 1966 season for Assateague's finest mares. Still, the little ponies loved by two or three generations of Americans aren't really the same as they originally were a few centuries ago, anyway.

There are several explanations of their origin on the lonely blowing islands. The story with the most mystery and appeal tells of the escape to the island of Moorish horses, from the wreck of a Spanish galleon which was transporting them to Peru to work in the gold mines. Since this supposedly occurred during the sixteenth century, the escapees would have had the same blood and breeding as the stock from which came the Andalusian of today.

However, if they were of that stock, they were probably the heavier and more hardy specimens, which would help to explain why they survived with such success up to the present.

Another popular legend claims that they were wandering Indian ponies (possibly Chickasaw Horses) seeking refuge from encroaching civilization on the sea-swept Assateague Island.

Whatever they originally were, it is said that they stood about 14 hands and were mostly soberly colored in black, brown, chestnut, and bay hues.

Through the years they were subjected to various whims in the way of outcrossing. Diminutive Shetlands decreased their size and produced outlandish pinto patterns which are predominant today. Welsh ponies turned among them also kept their size down, but contributed dapple-gray coats to the herds as well as a bit of class to their head carriage.

The pony breeding is very evident today in the heavy, sometimes potty bodies, medium to large heads, well-arched necks, and full, flowing manes and tails. The main colors seen are gray, sorrel, bay, black, and the predominant pinto coloration, which points up the tendency of a pinto parent and a plain-colored parent to produce a pinto foal.

During the next few years, the shape of the Chincoteague Ponies will very likely change drastically. From their present size of 12 to 13:2 hands, they will probably begin once again to occasionally reach 14 hands. Instead of being ponies, they may turn into real horses. Their heads will become finer and their bodies possibly more streamlined, and doubtless they will bring better prices at the annual Pony Pennings.

The Pony Pennings are an ancient tradition in themselves, and incidently, now a tremendous tourist attraction. They were initiated early in the 1700's by the residents of Chincoteague, who felt that all the fine horseflesh over on Assateague shouldn't be allowed to go to waste. The Chincoteague Volunteer Fire Department now hosts the Pony Penning Day on the last Thursday of July each year.

Chincoteague Island residents go by boat or horseback to Assateague Island, where the ponies live the year around under harsh conditions of hurricanes, storms, heat, and sandflies. There are twelve separate herds, each with its own stallion and ten to twelve mares and foals. Recently, helicopters have been used to speed the process of herding the elusive ponies to the south end of Assateague Island, where they are put in corrals, watered, and left to rest overnight.

When low tide comes the next morning, the ponies are driven into the water, which is by then about a quarter of a mile across. The horses are kept from escaping on the sides by lines of boats filled with enthusiastic islanders. Any foals younger than eight weeks are not made to swim the distance, but are carried across by boat. When the ponies emerge wet and glistening onto Chincoteague, they are funneled down the main street to the corrals at the other end.

The littlest foals, still unweaned, are then sold for from fifty to two hundred and fifty dollars, the proceeds going to the Fire Department to buy equipment. Sometimes the older foals and ponies find a buyer, too, before the ponies are herded back to their range on Assateague.

The pony foals are gentle and endearing, and many a tourist loses his heart and finds himself unexpectedly the fond owner of a sturdy little Chincoteague Pony foal which will need much milk and tender care until it can be weaned from the bottle.

The Chincoteague Pony of the future may be prettier than the pony of today, but the people who remember the spunky little ponies like Misty of Chincoteague will probably always be convinced that the old-time ponies were best of all.

Connemara Pony

Outstanding points of conformation:

HEIGHT: 13 to 14:2 hands.

COLORS AND MARKINGS: gray, black, bay, brown, dun, cream, and occasional roans and chestnuts. Pintos are not allowed. Some white markings are seen.

BODY: is compact, deep, and fairly long.

LEGS: are short, measuring seven to eight inches below the knee.

MANE AND TAIL: are long and fine; the tail is braided down from the top for several inches in typical hunting style, and the mane is also braided into eight to sixteen knots.

EYES: glass eyes are not permitted.

THE WORLD'S MOST POPULAR hunting and jumping pony is without any doubt the Irish Connemara. Unrivaled in jumping ability and stamina in the hunt field, it is strong enough to carry an adult with ease or a child in perfect safety. Its docility and gentleness fall into the category of the near-miraculous, for in its homeland of West Ireland, where it runs free and wild, its owner can capture it on the heath one day and take it, obediently following on the lead rope, to market the next day. This has been reported so often that it is hard to discount its authenticity. But in fact the whole story is even less likely than it seems at first glance.

The ponies have lived in a harsh environment for centuries. Their range is one of mountainous crags and bogs, boulders, heather, and gorse. There is a little green pasture, but the pickings are

lean. The ponies usually give birth in the shelter of the owner's stable, but after being foaled, the pony is turned out with its dam to mature and survive as best it can, and the inferior animals are automatically weeded out, for the winters are terrible, the feed poor, and the winds that blow off the Atlantic are wet and cold. Once a year, prior to the Connemara Pony Show, the owners begin to gather in the wild, untouched ponies. The task is such a difficult one amid the steep, rough terrain that the Connemara cowboys have learned over the years that the only way to trap the ponies is to force them into a bog. There the wild ponies get hopelessly mired and can be taken captive. If, after this traumatic experience, they can turn into meek, obedient ponies in a day or two, it is certainly a tribute to the breed!

The Connemara is the result of mixed ancestry. Centuries ago, the Irish pony in Connemara was probably much like the other ponies of Celtic stock to be found in northern Europe. When Ireland struck up a brisk commerce with Spain in the 1700's there was undoubtedly some introduction of Spanish Barbs and Jennets. And when the French joined forces with Ireland against England, they undoubtedly brought along their heavy-boned black horses. Arabian blood was infused numerous times to produce larger riding horses, and by the 1920's the Connemara was a confused pottage of every sort of horse that had ever been in Ireland. The Connemara Pony Breeders Society was formed in a last-ditch effort to save the valiant little Irish jumpers from being absorbed into all the breeds with which they had crossed. A group of mares and stallions with good characteristics were selected, and about a dozen of their progeny were turned out on the heath to survive as best they might. When they were gathered up two and a half years later, their numbers were fewer, but the ones that had survived were fleet runners, excellent jumpers, and had extremely hardy constitutions. Carefully controlled experiments introduced Thoroughbred, Irish Draft, and Arabian blood until the Society was satisfied with the results.

It is little wonder that Connemaras have intelligence, catlike balance, and great jumping ability, for without them, they could not survive. It can't be said that there is any particular type of conformation, even today, although good sloping shoulders, powerful hindquarters, tough feet, and excellent legs seem to be the Connemara's finer points, and its action is that of a horse, not a pony.

The Connemara was introduced to America in the early 1950's, and found immediate approval among those looking for an animal that would do just as good a job of hunting and jumping, but wasn't so large and often temperamental as the Thoroughbred. Since that time, the breed's growth has been phenomenal in more ways than one: its numbers have increased manyfold, but in some instances, probably due to better nutrition, so has its size. The large size has raised such a problem that the American Connemara Pony Society created a new section in the registry for ponies over 14:2 hands.

It is difficult to keep the Connemara inside fences, for it jumps for the sheer joy of jumping, often clearing obstacles half again as tall as itself. Its versatility makes it well suited for driving, dressage, and trail riding, as well as most other pony tasks. And, fortunately, the American Connemara Pony Society hasn't succumbed to the popular American habit of making a pony into what it isn't through the use of long hooves, artificial devices such as tail wigs or special shoes, and posing in a stretched position. Connemaras are shown as typical hunting ponies, often with a flash of colorful braid in the mane or tail, and standing naturally and easily.

Falabella Miniature Horse

Outstanding points of conformation:

HEIGHT: up to 7:2 hands, or 30 inches.

COLORS AND MARKINGS: all colors, Appaloosa coloring quite common. White markings usual.

GENERAL CONFORMATION: proportions are generally good; the Falabella and the Midget Shetlands are the only ponies of this size. By way of comparison, the Falabella usually has better conformation and is the only pony of its size with Appaloosa markings.

MANE AND TAIL: full and long.

WHILE THERE is little good to be said for the Midget Pony, there is a breed of tiny ponies which seems to bypass that category entirely and form a new one of its own. Called the Falabella Miniature Horse, it is the continuing product of more than a hundred years of patient line-breeding and outcrossing, and the result is very interesting. This pony has excellent conformation. Whereas the "quickie midget" pony is usually misshapen with enormous head in comparison to its size, malformed legs, and potty body, the Falabella has horselike proportions in a 120-pound body. It matures to no more than thirty inches, so the buyer can be certain his miniature horse won't shoot upward if he feeds it well.

The origin of the Falabella Miniature Horse is the ranch of Señor Julio Cesar Falabella in Argentina. For the past century, Señor Falabella, his father, grandfather, and great-grandfather

have bred smaller and ever smaller ponies in order to create the smallest breed of ponies. At one time they had a herd of four hundred perfect specimens, so one might concede that they were quite successful. Unfortunately, they didn't keep records, although they know that the main stock was Shetland, and it is possible that the Criollo and the short-legged Petizo, both Argentinian ponies, contributed to the breed. Some of the tiny ponies are marked with Appaloosa spots, and the donor of these certainly wasn't the Shetland!

It will probably be only a matter of years until the Falabella becomes fairly numerous in America. Señor Falabella has placed the price of mares at three thousand dollars, stallions at five thousand, and he might well be charging more by now, since prices are always subject to fluctuation and the original price was three hundred dollars. The high price doesn't seem to discourage prospective Falabella Horse owners, and import has been fairly steady. The pony seems to have first appeared here in the late fifties and early sixties, and since it matures at two years and has a life expectancy of about forty years, there should soon be sufficient progeny that some will become available within the United States.

The Falabella doesn't differ radically in its general makeup from the larger horse. It eats the same food, only less of it by far; it executes the same gaits; it can be turned out to pasture without special coddling; its gestation period is the same as for the larger animal; and it is, in addition, well accepted by larger horses. The very fact of its small size makes it useful for a unique role — the tiny stallion is used to "flirt" with the large mares to prepare them for breeding, but because of his small size he himself cannot mate with the mares.

A Falabella foal is delightful. No larger than a pup, it is featherweight and fragile, measuring only eight inches at the withers and weighing about a pound. The tiny foal can be cradled easily in one hand.

The decrease in size hasn't affected the Falabella's intelligence, except possibly to make it a little smarter than the average horse. Many an owner has spent just a few hours of time teaching his little miniature to shake hands, bow, and do other engaging tricks that would do credit to a high-school horse. The pony loves to jump, as a rule, and performing is one of its greatest joys. It will take leaps over obstacles as high as its head, and it will perform its gait on command with a minimum of instruction. Its nature is gentle and agreeable in nearly all cases, and it usually loves to romp with children as much as they enjoy romping with it. Large enough for a child up to eight years old to ride, the ponies are often used to pull small carts or carriages in Argentina, since an animal can always pull more weight than it can bear upon its back. All sorts of tack is made in Argentina for the Falabella Miniature Horse, but there are probably few, if any, places it can be obtained here. In the United States, the Falabella seems to be chiefly decorative and amusing, much like the poodle or St. Bernard. Proud owners keep them in the yard and welcome them into the house on occasion, and have even been known to pop them into the car for a trip downtown. The results of this practice are open to speculation, for how does one go about housebreaking a horse?

Gotland Pony

Outstanding points of conformation:

HEIGHT: 11 to 13 hands.

COLORS AND MARKINGS: all solid colors, including albino and palomino, but no pintos are found. Extensive white markings are uncommon, even on legs and face. Most common colors are black, bay, and brown, in that order.

FACE: profile of nose is wavy, there being one depression between the eyes and another midway down the nose. This is similar to the extinct Tarpan's profile.

CHESTNUTS: are sometimes missing.

CROUP: rounded but not steep, and the tail is well set.

MANE AND TAIL: full and long.

IN GOTLAND, an island province of Sweden, there is a creature which the inhabitants call a Skogsbagge. It generally is a dark-colored animal which grows a warm wooly coat in the winter and in some areas lives half-wild in the woods. The name means "forest buck" and the animal in question is quite as nimble and quick as a deer, with a lightness and elasticity seldom seen elsewhere. But another name it has is Skogsruss, meaning "forest horse," for this is the Gotland Pony — a pony in size, but by custom a horse. Its ancestors have lived on the island for possibly ten thousand years, as proven by Tarpan-like skeletons dug from prehistoric caves, and in all that time it has changed very little. In fact, its Tarpan ancestry can be seen quite clearly in the wavy face profile. Although kept pure by the isolation of the island in the north-

ern Baltic Sea, there has been some minor infusion of foreign blood which bears mentioning. To prevent excessive inbreeding, Welsh blood was introduced to provide an outcross line. Since the Welsh ponies chosen were not distinctly different in type or color, their effect on the breed's conformation and type was small. In the late 1800's, a half-oriental (some say Arabian) stallion from a native mare was used to increase the size. However, in addition to size, he introduced odd gray roan, blanket, and spotted coloration to his offspring. Fortunately, few if any of his line remain today. A half-Syrian pony in the early 1900's introduced dun color as well as intensifying the native trotting abilities, to produce a breed peculiarly suited to the trotting turf, making the Gotland the Standardbred of the pony world. In Gotland it is harness-raced by children up to seventeen years of age and has attained speeds of 3:04 minutes for the mile. Summer finds the ponies trotting on grass courses, while in winter they blithely speed on packed snow tracks. Unofficial world record for the breed was set by an eight-year-old mare and a twelve-year-old boy.

The Gotland Pony is probably put to the most miscellaneous uses of any pony. In Sweden it has been used on the farm, for cavalry purposes, jumping, pleasure riding, trot-harness racing, carriage racing, flat-gallop racing, dressage, and in teaching classes of youngsters to learn to ride, race, and care for their animals.

In the United States, where it has experienced tremendous increase in numbers since its debut in 1957, it is also being used for racing, but not always by children, as it is in Sweden. Its other uses are those which the Americans always apply their ponies to: pleasure, jumping, and just about anything else the pony can do.

For the last one hundred years, ever since the breed almost disappeared due to being shipped to the European continent for working in the mines, the Swedish government has inspected every Gotland Pony to apply for registration. Only the very best ponies are registered, and only the registered ponies have been imported to America.

The Gotland Pony is long-lived and fertile. Many have lived to be forty, and mares have been known to foal at the advanced age of thirty. In style, it approaches the horse, rather than the pony, ideal. Light and lively, it shows vigor and intelligence, and it is usually easily handled and trained. It is seldom known to have the common pony vices of kicking, biting, and stubbornness.

The Gotland Pony is a hard and willing worker. When the coach was a familiar sight in Gotland, the animals drawing it were the Gotland Ponies. One pony could pull around eight hundred pounds, but two were expected to pull better than a ton. They often traveled thirty-five miles at a stretch, a formidable distance for even a large draft horse pulling such a heavy load as a coach.

The American Gotland Horse Association is one of the most active breed registries in the United States. Although the numbers of the Gotland Pony are yet fairly small, the information about them is readily available in leading horse magazines, 4-H literature, and numerous brochures prepared by the organization.

As in Sweden, the owners here have avoided the trend to fit their animals, and they keep them in their natural condition most of the year. It may be that as the numbers of Gotland Ponies increase in the United States and as Gotland shows and sales come into being, there will be more tendency to trim them, because they look quite as much like forest rams, or possibly even bears, as ponies in their winter coats.

Hackney Pony

Outstanding points of conformation:

HEIGHT: up to 14:2 hands.

COLORS AND MARKINGS: bay, brown, or black. White markings are fairly common.

EARS: small and pointed well forward.

EYES: bright, bold, and prominent.

NOSE: generally roman-nosed in a refined way.

WITHERS: tend to be flattish, but since the Hackney Pony is seldom ridden this is not a serious fault.

MANE AND TAIL: the mane and tail are naturally long and flowing. There are two divisions of Hackney Pony. If it is a Cob-tail, the tail is docked to six inches and the mane is in fourteen plaits. If it is a Long-tail, it is shown with flowing mane and tail.

THE HACKNEY HORSE is the only American horse that has ever regained its popularity by diminishing to pony size, and it has succeeded quite grandly. Both the horse and pony are of the same breeding except that there has been an infusion of Welsh, Shetland, and Fell Pony blood to create the pony-size Hackney. The two are registered together, but the pony makes up nearly 95 percent of the numbers registered.

As with nearly any breed, the smaller individual is likely to have better form than the larger. With the Hackney Pony, this is particularly true. The pony is strictly a show pony, and bred for one purpose only — that of performing as a show harness pony. To this end, it is taught only two gaits, a lively walk and a flashy trot,

and it is seldom ridden, jumped, or raced (although it is an excellent jumper and fast) for the simple reason that it is very uncomfortable to ride due to its high, spirited action.

The spectacular gaits are exciting to watch, and the pony reaches so high that it seems to defy gravity. Naturally enough, the ponies with the highest action are the most valuable, sometimes bringing huge sale prices. The legs are lifted almost violently, flung forward fluidly and extravagantly, and at the height of the action there is a slight pause which reminds the spectator of a Pegasus about to take off — then they are lowered to the ground swiftly and with precision, ready for the next stride. The hocks are very strong in the Hackney Pony, and are folded neatly under the body with each step, the hind hock nearly striking the belly, the front knee almost on a level with the pony's chin. This is the ideal action, of course, and not all Hackney Ponies can reach such perfection. But those that do are by far the most popular and in demand.

Neither the Hackney Pony nor the Hackney Horse is born with such exaggerated movement. The tendency is there, as it is in very few other breeds, but the end product is the result of months and years of intensive training. To strengthen the legs before training commences, the trainer puts a wooden-bead anklet on each leg. The pony dislikes these noisy, heavy anklets and spends a good deal of time trying to kick them off. The object of the anklets is to strengthen the legs, and they do an admirable job.

Skillful shoeing is a must, as are long hooves. Both long hooves and heavy shoes tend to make the pony lift its legs higher, for in taking a stride it must work extra hard to lift the foot, and at the top of the action the extra force throws the foot higher and farther forward. But such aids aren't all that give a pony good movement. Without expert bitting, training, and driving, the pony will not develop to its full capacity. Handled by a novice, it will give a poor showing, no matter how well prepared it is.

Part of the Hackney Pony's brilliant appearance is dependent upon its collected stance. Its neck is arched, its nose is tucked in, its tail is raised alertly, and its body is slim and taut; every movement is an exercise in grace and style. Many of these traits are a triumph of toil. The neck arch and tucked nose are the result of constant application of the checkrein, loose in the beginning and tightened little by little as more suppleness is shown. The tail is made to stand up in much the same way. The slim underline is achieved by keeping the pony on a high protein diet, and a leather or plastic hood sweats a meaty neck or shoulders into trim lines. In fact, the Hackney undergoes most of the disciplines dealt to the American Saddle Horse.

Hackney Ponies are fitted either with docked tail and braided mane or with long flowing mane and tail. The difference depends upon whether they will be shown in Hackney classes or Harness Pony classes. The Harness Pony's mane and tail are left in the natural state except that the tail is trained to arch upward. The pony in the Hackney class has its tail docked to a length of about six inches and its mane is braided into fourteen tight little knobs.

The Hackney Pony is most definitely not a child's pony. It is an expensive toy to be handled with the greatest skill and precision, for it requires adult maturity and long years of experience to get the fantastic results demanded of the vibrant, exciting Hackney Pony.

Icelandic Pony

Outstanding points of conformation:

HEIGHT: 11 to 13 hands.

COLORS AND MARKINGS: chestnut, gray, black, palomino, pinto, and dun (sometimes with silver mane and tail). Some of the colors turn white in the winter, the mane and tail staying the same year around.

HEAD: fairly heavy.

NECK: short and sturdy, but well carried.

HINDQUARTERS: sloping, muscular and very strong.

MANE AND TAIL: thick and heavy. The forelock is very long, so Icelanders hack it off straight, giving the ponies bangs.

THE ICELANDIC PONY is the European answer to the five-gaited American Saddle Horse. In fact, it preceded the American Saddle Horse by a good many years. For, in addition to the flat walk, trot, and canter, many hardy little Icelandic Ponies can step into a flowing pace or a ground-covering running walk (called the *tolt* in Iceland) on command.

At first glance, the Icelandic Pony doesn't seem very captivating. Its neck is short and a little thick, the hindquarters are sloping and muscular, its head is heavy, the jaws and teeth deep (sometimes with tooth roots as long as three inches) and strong for grinding the tough grass and twigs that make up its diet. Since the Icelandic Pony must breathe in quantities of frigid air, its nose is large and blunt with big nasal cavities. A more delicate nose would be pret-

tier, certainly, but the nasal cavities of, for instance, the Arabian Horse, wouldn't begin to warm the icy air. The animal would be very prone to pneumonia and frosted lungs, which wouldn't be conducive to long life. And the Icelandic Ponies are known for their long and productive lives — an Icelandic mare, Tulle, died in 1954 at the age of fifty-seven! Many of these ponies are used for packing and trekking until well into their thirties.

Trekking is a traditional Icelandic pastime, also practiced to a lesser extent in some northern European countries such as Sweden and Norway. Groups of men, women, and children strike off across the countryside for sheer enjoyment of the exercise and scenery. They ride the best and most comfortable ponies, and pack the other ponies with as much as 220 pounds of gear and supplies. Twenty to forty miles might be traveled during a day, and at night the ponies graze the wild pastures and catch as much sleep as they can before dawn and another trekking day begins. The ponies apparently thrive under these conditions, being the only breed of pony fully acclimated to a year-round semiarctic environment.

About half of the ponies in Iceland run in a half-wild state in the open untended pastures with scarcely any shelter, sometimes none. Their hardiness is a result of a thousand years of natural selection and stringent weeding by the ruthless near-arctic conditions. Geologically speaking, Iceland is still a young island. In the mid-1700's, a great volcanic eruption drastically reduced the numbers of ponies already decimated by extraordinarily harsh winters en-

countered in the previous five centuries. It is said that in the worst winters the ponies have been known to wait on the beach for fish to be washed ashore so that they can retrieve and eat them. For this reason, they are sometimes referred to as Fisher Ponies.

Their ancestors were Scandinavian and British ponies brought by the immigrants during the first great waves of migration to Iceland between A.D. 900 and A.D. 1100. These ponies were of Celtic stock, probably closely resembling the Norwegian Dun of today. It is claimed that little or no foreign blood was introduced since A.D. 1100, and if this is so, then it is indeed a pure breed. Such claims do seem to be borne out by breeding results, for Icelandic Pony blood is highly prepotent and when crossed with other breeds, its strong attributes of docility, stamina, and willingness show up quite clearly in the offspring, as do its physical characteristics.

There are about thirty thousand Icelandic Ponies in Iceland, and the numbers are growing steadily in the United States. Everyone who sees these game little ponies comes away with enthusiastic reports or even one of the ponies itself. It isn't as difficult to find one here now as it once was, for many importations have been made and the herds in the United States have increased enough so that importation isn't necessary.

Since trekking isn't really an American sport — the nearest thing being camping trips and trail rides — the Icelandic Pony has become popular in other fields here as well. Some have been in use for a time now in Colorado and Wyoming as cutting horses and for general stock work. Others have found favor with youngsters for gymkhana events, showing good speed and nimble footwork. Since the ponies have more the build of a short-legged horse than a pony, they provide a comfortable seat for adults as well as children.

Midget Pony

Outstanding points of conformation:

HEIGHT: usually below 9 hands, or 36 inches. The definitions are variable.

COLORS AND MARKINGS: all colors except Appaloosa markings. White markings common.

GENERAL CONFORMATION: conformation seems to be overlooked in the search for small size. Midget Ponies are sometimes without any redeeming features but smallness. There have been some good Midget Ponies, but even with them, the head is usually much oversized and the body is dumpy.

MANE AND TAIL: often thick and nearly to the ground (this is not unusual since the whole pony is nearly to the ground).

MIDGET PONIES usually derive from Shetland stock, produced by breeding a particularly small pony to another particularly small pony. The resulting progeny is often as small or smaller than either parent. This is reasonable and legitimate, but there are some factors which often enter into the Midget Pony business that have given it a very bad name in an equally short time.

Good small ponies are hard to find. If a pony owner is breeding for midgets, he often starts out with only one or two ponies and

124

isn't careful enough about breeding lines. Consequently, in far too many cases, subsequent offspring of the original pair are mated with each other and to the original stud or mare to such an extent that the resulting Midget Ponies (admittedly much smaller than the original two) have a vastly higher chance of being defective. The chances of producing freak foals are increased because recessive genes are doubled and tripled. It is not uncommon for a midget mare to die during delivery of a normal-size foal, or to have to be aided by caesarian section. These faults can sometimes be lessened by introducing new blood into the breeding program through a different small pony, but then, this usually increases the size (since really small ponies are so rare), so it generally isn't done frequently enough. Results of inbreeding can be internal deformity as well as external, so that some Midget Ponies are drastically defective although they may look perfectly "normal."

Another factor, poor nutrition, is sometimes used to bilk the public. Consider a fictional Mr. Jones selling Mr. Smith a twenty-six-inch Midget Pony with the claim that the pony has obviously reached its full growth since it is three years old. Imagine Mr. Smith's chagrin and dismay when his "full-grown Midget" adds another four inches to its height in short order. What has happened? Mr. Jones, alas, neglected to tell Mr. Smith that the pony had been kept on a very scanty diet with poor nutrition to keep him from growing, and that when Mr. Smith lovingly and bounteously fed his new pony grain and sweet clover it naturally put on weight and height. Under Mr. Jones's care it wouldn't have gotten any taller, but it would have gone through life underfed and hungry. We must deduce that Mr. Jones was just a little unscrupulous, and although there are some fine exceptions, this is a common practice among Midget Pony breeders. There are two ways around this problem which a person wanting a tiny pony can take. He can either check up on the Mr. Joneses very carefully and talk to people who have bought from them, or be prepared to stint the pony's feed. The latter, however, is a cruel practice and certainly isn't recommended.

Ponies only twenty inches high have been recorded, and this is a unique size indeed. Desirable conformation is generally disregarded when breeding for small size, and the Midget Ponies raised in the United States seldom have well-proportioned conformation. Speed of production is much to blame, for breeders want tiny ponies immediately and sacrifice form and beauty for size. A large head is common (it is the large head which causes so much trouble during birth) as are poor legs. Midget Ponies are usually not exceptionally long-lived and their use is naturally limited by their size. Most are kept for decoration only, although they can support a very small child. They are useful for keeping a small lawn mowed, and some people with only a backyard still like to have a horse around the place. And for this purpose, a Midget Pony fills the bill beautifully.

Pony of the Americas

Outstanding points of conformation:

HEIGHT: 11:2 to 13:2 hands.

COLORS AND MARKINGS: those Appaloosa patterns common to the Appaloosa, including particolored skin around mouth and nostrils and on reproductive organs, and striped hooves.

FACE: straight or slightly dished.

TAIL: set high on croup.

MANE AND TAIL: not as spare as Appaloosa. Trimmed in the western style.

THE PONY OF THE AMERICAS, or as it is more popularly known, the POA, is something new. It is a pony manufactured to fill a specific niche — that of a large western using pony for the older child. It is quite appealing in two respects: first, its flashy Appaloosa coloring, and second, its conformation which, if it meets the ideal, is a cross between the Arabian and the Quarter Horse. To further the western image, it is trimmed and ridden western style and is never shown in the stretched stance. Its action is low, as is most practical for a using horse, and to this end, it is shod with either light plates or no shoes at all.

At present the conformation of the POA is various, but it will naturally solidify when the registry is closed to foundation stock of

unknown and miscellaneous breeding. The Association plans to partially close the stud books in 1970, so that at least one parent must be a registered POA. The POA foundation stock is indistinguishable from and often actually is National Appaloosa Pony stock, and vice versa. During the formative years, the POA has borrowed characteristics from many pony and horse breeds. Shetland and Welsh ponies have contributed small size; Arabian, Quarter Horse, and Thoroughbred have mainly contributed style and conformation; and, naturally, the Appaloosa Horse and Pony have contributed style and the beautiful color patterns.

No pinto or albino breeding is allowed, and no pony is eligible if it has white stockings above the knees or hocks, or a bald face which covers any portion of the side of the head, since these signs indicate pinto breeding. In order to quickly increase the number of POA's, some breeders mate their POA stallions to solid-color mares to produce spotted foals. Since the spotting factor is so predominant, the get of these progeny are usually also spotted.

The markings of a Pony of the Americas must be recognizable at forty feet, and this requirement often gives the breeder some anxious times, for nearly 30 percent of all POA foals are a solid color at birth with only white sclera giving promise of spots to come (this is true of all Appaloosa-marked horses). The bright colors

sometimes don't materialize for as long as three years after birth.

One POA, Corette's Scottish Chieftain #18, has such a reputation for siring loud color that his admirers have founded an auxiliary association for his get. This isn't a separate registry, however, but a registry within a registry.

The POA's are very popular racing ponies. Although they may not stand over 13:2 hands, the fastest ones are setting records only about two seconds slower than the times of full-sized Quarter Horses. This remarkable speed also makes them favorites for such gymkhana events as barrel racing and pole bending, as well as calf or goat roping and cutting. And in a little slower and more prosaic manner, they make perfect farm and ranch horses for general pleasure riding and trail rides.

This evolution of this breed is interesting because of its tremendous growth rate and degree of acceptance as a separate and distinct breed. The foundation sire, Black Hand #1, was a pure white stallion with black diamond markings over his loin, croup, and back. His dam was an Appaloosa, but his sire was a Shetland, and his personality, size, and color so captured the imagination of his owner, Leslie Boomhower, of Mason City, Iowa, that in 1954 Mr. Boomhower began a registry with Black Hand as the nucleus; over the years the numbers have soared with no decrease of growth in sight. The demand for them has spilled over into Canada and South America, as well as several overseas countries.

It is possible to find a POA priced to fit almost any means. Geldings often go for two to three hundred dollars if they are of good quality, and top breeding mares and stallions have brought prices into five figures at public sale. Some private sales are said to have gone well above eight thousand dollars. For those with limited finances, a foal can often be purchased for a lower price, and the joy of raising it will be an additional bonus.

Shetland Pony

Outstanding points of conformation:

HEIGHT: up to 11:2 hands.

COLORS AND MARKINGS: all solid colors, albino and pinto included, but no Appaloosa markings. Silver dapple and gold dapple are among its prettier shades. White markings common. Any eye color.

FACE: is straight or slightly dished.

EARS: short and fine.

NECK: long and fine; stallions have strong crest.

MANE AND TAIL: full and long, but not bushy. Show animals have tails set, mane and tail flowing.

THE SHETLAND PONY of present-day America bears only faint resemblance to its British forebears. The size is roughly the same, although American breeders sometimes overshoot the mark (and a place is understandingly provided for such oversize ponies in the American registry). The rest of the pony has become streamlined, much to the horror and disgust of British Shetland enthusiasts, and there is little common ground between the two.

The Shetland is one of the really ancient breeds. It is said that the Norsemen carried little northern ponies to the Shetland Isles as long as two thousand years ago in their Viking ships. The ponies were larger then, but the rigorous life on the windswept islands made survival of smaller ponies more likely. Thus, through this ruthless weeding out by the elements, only tiny ponies of about ten hands evolved to be the pony we know today. When feed is increased, however, the animals tend to be above average in size.

The Shetland Islands are found about two hundred miles north of Scotland. The terrain is barren and rocky, and grass is so scarce that sometimes the ponies are driven to eating seaweed. Temperatures are consistently low, and mist and stormy weather are prevalent. The Shetland Pony has some defense, for it has long, fine hair which mats when it gets wet to provide a weatherproof shield. Its mane is long and thick, often falling profusely on both sides of the neck. The thickness of the mane protects the ears and eyes of the pony in bad weather.

Traditionally, the Shetland Pony has been firmly knit and heavy. Until the mid-1800's it was used as a riding pony and carried heavy loads of peat to be used as fuel in the crofters' homes. But around the middle of the nineteenth century, the Shetland became important in the coal mines of Great Britain, pulling coal carts averaging twelve hundred pounds through the dark mine tunnels.

When electricity came into common use, the job of the coal-mine pony ended, and Shetland Ponies emerged as pets and children's riding steeds. Their shape was improved upon slightly as breeders began to look for riding quality. They made minor outcrosses to Icelandic Pony and Arabian to increase size and style, but the impact was limited. In time, the Shetland came into the show ring, and for these events, their British owners, to this day, show them in natural form. They are prepared about as much as American breeders prepare a draft horse. They feed it until it is very nearly fat, leave its tail unset and untrimmed, the forelock long and bushy, and the hooves naturally short. In fact, the pony very much resembles a draft horse with its large head, short, thick neck, round body

with well-sprung ribs, full quarters, and short, strong legs. But then, this is only natural since heavy work and big loads have always been the Shetland's lot.

The British are sentimental in some ways. They wouldn't think of drastically changing the shape of their little Shetland because they've grown fond of it that way. But its numbers become fewer and fewer — the Shetland numbers less than a thousand in its homeland. The torch has been taken up by America, and the wick trimmed and altered, until the pony, although still called a Shetland (and in kid-pony circles is still a chunky little animal) sometimes looks much more like a miniature American Saddle Horse than a child's pet.

The change in America's Shetland was a gradual thing, starting in the late 1800's. The pony was never used for heavy draft in the United States, except in a minor role of pulling children's carts. The need was for a flashy buggy pony for small tasks (like running down to the store for a package of pins) for which it would be impractical to hitch up the big horse and carriage. The refinement was natural and gradual, without the influence of outside blood, and the change was making itself visible by 1900. Unfortunately, the bicycle came into being and squashed this innovation.

But the switch had already been made, and the slimmer Shetland was a prettier pony and it was easier for a child to wrap his legs around this new type than around the old-fashioned round-barreled Shetland, so the change remained and intensified. For even if the bicycle and later the auto did outclass the pony and the pony cart, the kids clamored for a pony — and even in today's grossly mechanical age, they still do.

There are two types of Shetland in the United States today, just as there are probably two types of nearly any breed: the show animal and the pet. The pet Shetland in America resembles Britain's show Shetland rather closely. But the show Shetland in America is a flashy, very nearly untouchable, bit of royalty. It is fitted to the highest degree, and lives on what a British Shetland would consider a starvation diet. Its forelock is trimmed and beribboned, its tail is trained to make it appear to be set, its hooves are grown very long and shod with heavy shoes to give the pony high action. Perhaps the most telling comment on the change in style and conformation is that an imported British Shetland may not be registered in the American Stud Book even though it may be a registered Shetland of the highest caliber in the British Isles.

There is little importing done these days, anyway. Americans seem to prefer what they have, and the British have no particular wish to export their remaining few. The early days of shipping exerted great losses among the ponies, for there was little of our modern knowledge about sanitation and protection against disease and injury. In fact, it was thought that ponies on shipboard contracted lockjaw (tetanus) from being frightened by rough deck hands!

One of the reasons for the Shetland's great popularity today in America is its adoption by the 4-H Club program. The youngsters have the Shetlands as projects, raise and train them with loving care, and learn horsemanship and sportsmanship along the way. They have an opportunity to meet competition each summer at the 4-H Fairs, and often the best projects go on to the state fairs. This is not only excellent for the children, but good publicity for the ponies, also, since it points up their docile, loving natures and abilities in the show ring. Even stallions are safely handled by the children.

The people who handle Shetland Ponies at big horse shows aren't usually children. This has brought about the peculiar result of turning the show Shetland almost exclusively into a roadster or harness pony as far as exhibiting purposes are concerned. It isn't that the ponies aren't capable of carrying adults — to the contrary, they easily carry half their own weight and could perform this task readily. Apparently, adults don't feel at home on them, so there is no call for such performance classes. Competition runs high, however, in roadster and harness divisions and in halter classes where they are walked and trotted in hand then stretched to their utmost to stand for inspection. The turnout at these shows is tremendous, for there are an estimated seventy-four thousand Shetlands at present in the United States.

Another growing spectator sport is pony trotting races. The Shetland can also be trained to pace with the correct schooling and shoeing. It is fascinating to watch these miniature racers pulling tiny sulkies in which are ensconced comparatively huge drivers. One interesting note is that the sulky racers are usually ponies that have previously trained as roadster or harness ponies to show flashy action and flexion. They tend to waste energy and sacrifice speed in using so much excessive movement, whereas it is noticed that the successful Standardbred trotters are confirmed "daisy-cutters," lifting their feet just enough to clear the ground and concentrating all their energy into forward movement. This phase of pony use is growing rapidly, both in number of competitors and spectator appeal. A more rustic sport gaining favor is chuckwagon racing, in which ponies pull wooden wagons in hitches of four and six ponies. At some state fairs, Shelties (as they are sometimes called) engage in weight-pulling contests. They are exceptionally strong for their size, pulling up to three times their own weight. This, perhaps, is just a further indication of the Shetland's hardy constitution. For its size, it must be acknowledged as the strongest of all horse breeds. In addition, Shetlands are noted for their longevity, living sturdy, useful lives long past the life span of most other breeds.

The American Shetland Pony Club, organized in 1888, is the only registry for Shetlands in the United States. Its breed requirements seem most generous. One of its more unexpected disqualifications is the rejection of roman-nosed specimens.

As the human population explosion makes itself felt in the not so distant future, the tiny Shetland will very likely be one of the breeds to suffer least from the subsequent shortage of space — for the Shetland fits in where there is no room at all for a horse.

Welsh Pony

Outstanding points of conformation:

HEIGHT: 11 to 14 hands. Build is that of miniature coach horse.
COLORS AND MARKINGS: all solid colors, pinto not found. Grey and chestnut are most popular. White markings common.
HEAD: small and tapering to muzzle, similar to Arabian Horse's.
EARS: small, pointed.
MANE AND TAIL: tail set well, carried high. Mane and tail left long and flowing except where pony is used for western or hunting classes, then the appropriate fitting is applied.

THE WELSH PONY is one of the most popular and best established pony breeds in the United States. In the 1880's small numbers of Welsh Ponies were imported into Illinois, and in 1907 the Welsh Pony and Cob Society of America was established to register American ponies.

Until recent times in the United States, only the small Welsh Mountain Pony could be found in any numbers, although an occasional Welsh Cob might be discovered in out-of-the-way places (the British name "Cob," referring to a large pony of riding and driving type, was dropped from the Society's name in 1946 because it is not in common use in America). The Mountain Pony was prized for its small size, intermediate between the horse and Shetland Pony, and its miniature coach horse build. Those who wanted a larger pony than the Welsh Mountain Pony simply crossed it with a horse. The results were quite unpredictable, however, the cross sometimes far exceeding pony standards. In recent years there has been an upsurge of interest in the large

size Welsh Riding Pony (formerly the Welsh Cob), for it is the ideal stylish intermediate mount for the older child.

The Welsh Pony Society Stud Book registers the Welsh Pony under two sections: Section A ponies stand 12:2 hands or under and are called Welsh Mountain Ponies or just plain Welsh Ponies. Section B ponies are called Welsh Riding Ponies and stand 12:3 to 14 hands. Unlike the American Stud Book, the British Stud Book divides the Section A ponies at 12 hands and the Section B ponies between 12:1 and 13:2 hands; but since the Welsh Pony usually matures one or two inches taller in the United States, it was felt that some allowance should be made for this fact.

If the Welsh Pony were to be compared to other horse breeds, it would show the most resemblance to the Arabian. Perhaps this is because there is a good bit of Arabian blood in its lineage. There are also moderate amounts of Hackney and Thoroughbred, which tend to give style and character to the little Welsh Pony.

When the Romans conquered Wales they brought their own horses with them, and since they stayed several hundred years there was undoubtedly quite a bit of interbreeding. This early crossing of oriental horses on the northern ponies gave the Welsh a head start on looks and carriage. Its personality is very gentle, and this, plus its alertness, makes it relatively easy to train. It is agile from its heritage of living among the rocks and crags of Wales, and it is especially hardy since only the best ponies could survive the elements and terrain. The ponies were hounded by bounty hunters under the edict of King Henry VIII (all horses under 15 hands must be destroyed). Evidently he felt the small

ponies to be a threat to the breeding of large horses useful for agriculture and war. The Welsh Ponies managed to escape by eluding hunters in the ravines and rough country where few other horses could go.

After the threat from King Henry VIII had passed, the Welsh Pony once more became the favorite horse (at least, they once more dared to admit it publicly without fear of the king's wrath) of the Welshmen. It worked faithfully in the coal mines and between cart shafts, and carried the big farmer to market on its back with no seeming effort. In addition, it influenced the early formation of the Hackney, hunter, polo pony, and some claim that its blood is present in early English Thoroughbred breeding. It is used quite extensively today to produce medium- and lightweight hunters. The usual cross is Thoroughbred sire to Welsh dam, and the result is an active and sure-footed little horse with good jumping ability. Many hunters and jumpers shown in open competition by children and small adults are this combination, for the small person feels more at home on his own size horse, and find grooming and saddling simpler.

In America, both the Welsh Mountain Pony and the Welsh Riding Pony have carved quite a niche for themselves in such areas as sulky racing, harness, dressage, halter, hunting and jumping, and as a child's western pony. In Britain it is shown at halter in a natural state, unstretched and with short feet; and it is usually shown this way in the United States, although more and more showing is done in the long-hoofed, stretched, Saddle Horse style. The distinctive trot of the Welsh Pony is beautiful. It has been described as a "daisy-cutting" gait, and were the pony to trot through a field of daisies, it would indeed cut them neatly off. Many Welsh are trained to do a high, showy trot, and all too likely the day will come when there will be an impossibly wide gap between the backyard Welsh Pony and the show pony, as there is between the two kinds of Shetlands. This is truly unfortunate, for the Welsh Pony has a special natural presence and action which, like breathtaking scenery, is far better left unimproved.

Draft Horses

THE DRAFT HORSE is designed principally for heavy pulling, and to this end its conformation is blocky and compact, short-legged, and extremely well muscled. The Clydesdale is bred for its action at the walk and trot as well. It is inaccurate to say that the draft horse "pulls" the load, for it does not pull; it pushes. To move the load it pushes on the collar, and the collar and various straps pull the load. Therefore the horse must be heavy enough to lean into the collar strongly enough to make the load move forward, while also maintaining its footing and forward momentum.

The draft horse isn't made for speed, and it is seldom asked to do more than a trot, for it is usually pulling something that would not stand up under being pulled at a gallop or even a brisk trot. So the speed mechanisms aren't developed in the draft horse. Nearly all its developments are heavy bone and muscle, and the average draft horse has the following conformation:

Points of conformation:

HEIGHT AND WEIGHT: 16 to 18 hands; 1700 to 2000 pounds.

HEAD: fairly lean, wide between the eyes, and a proper size for the body.

EARS: medium size and alert.

EYES: prominent and bright (most draft horses look sleepy).

PROFILE: this varies widely with the breed.

MUZZLE: nostrils large, lips firm and not pendulous.

JAW: big and round.

NECK: strong and muscular, more crested in stallions than in mares and geldings.

SHOULDERS: shorter and straighter than the saddle horse's. Too short a shoulder should be avoided because the concussion may injure foot, knee, and shoulder. If the shoulder is too sloped, the collar will not rest properly on it, and it will bind.

CHEST: deep and broad, with plenty of room for lungs.

FOREARM: medium length, with full complement of muscles, but needn't be especially bulky, for the front legs mainly bear weight.

KNEES: should be large and square.

CANNONS, FORE AND REAR: strong and short.

FETLOCKS, FORE AND REAR: should be large and square.

PASTERNS, FORE AND REAR: short, very strong, medium slope.

HOOVES, FORE AND REAR: should be large, round, and open to provide strong, large base from which horse works.

UNDERLINE: well let down, girth being large, and belly sufficiently large to sustain working horse's digestive needs.

RIBS: well sprung, making body look round and full.

BACK: short and very broad.

LOIN OR COUPLING: broad and well muscled.

CROUP: fairly long and level, well muscled, smoothly rounded.

HIP: good muscling, firm.

THIGH AND GASKIN: somewhat bulging with muscle. This is the widest part of the horse, and its source of power.

HOCK: a large joint, and square.

MANE AND TAIL: tail is nicely attached, mane and tail hair are long and thick, sometimes kinky. The draft horse usually has a docked tail.

FEATHER: hair on backs of legs varies with breed.

Belgian

HEIGHT AND WEIGHT: average height 16:1 hands; weight about 2000 pounds. Body short, very wide, and deep.

COLORS AND MARKINGS: roan, chestnut, bay most common; brown, gray, and black are sometimes seen. White markings small if any.

HEAD: medium size, squarish.

CROUP: generally sloping more than most draft breeds.

MANE AND TAIL: mane is often roached, tail docked at about six inches.

FEATHER: very little, much less than Clydesdale and Shire.

NOT TOO MANY YEARS ago, it appeared that the Belgian, along with the other draft horses, was doomed to a fairly swift extinction. The tractor seemed invincible, the workhorse appeared comparatively useless, and the Belgian's numbers started to decline. No longer did the rolling fields reverberate under its willing hoofbeats on farm after farm across the nation. No longer did its muscles roll, while great logs groaned and moved as it hauled them through the woods on mountain after mountain. And no more did cobblestones clatter as it pulled the heaviest carts down city streets in town after town. It became a rare sight, a horse to point out excitedly to the children and grandchildren, saying, "Look! That's the kind of horse that we used to farm with before the tractor came along!"

The Belgian nearly disappeared, but in a few remote spots there were still people who recognized its merits and proper uses. Those people kept the breed alive, and now it is starting to grow again.

Some people use Belgians for pulling fancy wagons at fairs, parades, and expositions, as advertisement for their products. Disneyland uses Belgians to draw brightly painted old-fashioned carriages and wagons. But the work that some other people are giving them is even more exciting, for it proves that Belgians have fought a battle and won it: they are once more used on some farms and dairies in their original capacity — that of plowing, planting, harvesting, and hauling. The Cheatham Dairy of Laveen, Arizona, is one of the best examples. Their Belgian and Suffolk Punch draft horses are used for such diverse jobs as cutting hay, pulling hay balers, preparing fields, and hauling hay wagons. The dairy has figures to prove that horses cost 25 percent less to maintain than tractors.

The Belgian is well adapted to farm work. It is compact in the extreme, usually being shorter than the Shire but weighing just as much. It moves well at both the walk and trot, although it is so wide that it rolls a little at the walk and wings slightly at both gaits. It is low to the ground, and this gives it an advantage in long, slow pulling. But the Belgian hasn't always been a drafter, and once it looked far different from this.

It is said that the Belgian Draft Horse evolved from Belgium's mighty destrier, which was called the Horse of Flanders or Flemish Horse, and was the war-horse of the Middle Ages. It bore the knights and Crusaders with ease, which is saying quite a lot, for with armor on both horse and rider weighing nearly four hundred pounds and the man's weight of about 140 to 250 pounds, this was no mean feat.

The Horse of Flanders was large and black, with a truly marvelous amount of hair and a sluggish disposition. When knighthood went out of fashion, the destrier was diverted into agriculture, where it was altered somewhat to make it more efficient. The later addition of Clydesdale, Percheron, and Shire blood helped to refine it and added various colors to its standard black. The Belgian was used solely for agriculture on Belgium farms until recent times, being the only type of horse bred there (lighter horses had to be brought in from surrounding countries if needed). Unfortunately for the breed, in Belgium today one of its chief uses is as tender, edible horsemeat, and to this end some of the finest and fattest young stock is sent.

Around 1900, a certain practice designed to increase the girth and size of the Belgian was used. By day, the foal was confined to a dark stable with nothing to do but eat grain and more grain, but at night, it was turned out to rich pastures to eat its fill. This procedure was continued until the animal was three years old, at which time it was broken to harness and worked normal daylight hours. Whether or not this really succeeded is open to question.

The Belgian Draft Horse began to appear sporadically in the United States in the late 1800's and in great numbers in the first decade of this century. At first, only stallions were imported, for use on native mares, but later, Belgian mares were also brought over in an attempt to further the breed in the United States. The Belgian Draft Horse Corporation of America was formed in 1887 to register the horses, and under its jurisdiction, the Belgian Draft

Horse was made considerably smoother and more refined. In 1917, the great imported stallion Farceur 7332 was bought for $47,500, a tremendous price for those times. The Belgian's great strength is unmatched; a recent world record in weight pulling was made by a pair of Belgians, their effort registering 4275 pounds on the dynamometer.

Cleveland Bay

Outstanding points of conformation:

HEIGHT AND WEIGHT: 16 to 17 hands; 1350 to 1550 pounds.
COLORS AND MARKINGS: always bay with black mane, tail, and lower legs. White markings confined to small star on forehead or none at all.
HEAD: well set, plain, but similar to Thoroughbred's.
NECK: long.
BODY: midway in weight between light horse and drafter.
LEGS: short.
MANE AND TAIL: usually left long and flowing.
FEATHER: very little.

THE SIGHT OF a hitch of big bays pulling a coach at a sturdy swinging trot is one of those things people nostalgically read about and maybe even long for when the freeways get clogged with noisy, smelly traffic so slow that a team of horses could certainly make as good or better time. But those days are past, and those coaches are gone, and so, too, are most of the durable Cleveland Bays that pulled them in the range states of the Old West.

The roads then were dusty trails, and the loads were heavy. Draft horses simply weren't usable, for they could not put forth sustained speed, even though they could pull quite a lot. The need was for a strong horse with tough legs, spirit and animation, and the ability to stand hot weather. The Cleveland Bay filled the bill perfectly, and it had the added advantage of always being bay, making matched teams a byword.

There are few Cleveland Bays left. The western states still have a few, and Virginia claims some. They are used mainly to produce heavyweight hunters through crossing with Thoroughbreds, a custom followed in England and the United States since the early 1800's. While the need for heavyweight hunters hasn't noticeably declined in the past few years, the breeders have found that they can make larger profits by breeding purebred Thoroughbreds as hunters and they have let crossbreeding of the Cleveland Bay slide.

This is truly unfortunate, for the Cleveland Bay is an ancient breed with a varied history. It began its career as a pack horse.

During the sixteenth and seventeenth centuries in England, there were no roads between most of the smaller towns and villages. Travelers went either on foot or on horseback, and if there was a burden to carry, it had to be carried either on their own backs or on the horses' backs. Enterprising merchants overcame the problems of transporting goods by producing a satisfactory pack horse and driving it from town to town loaded with goods. Medieval drawings portray these heavily burdened pack ponies and their masters. Ponies though they were, they were the forerunners of the Cleveland Bay, and through them quite a thriving business burgeoned. In the 1690's, a scheduled packtrain ran between London and Exeter carrying pots and pans, seed, silks, and wool, and various things outlying communities relied upon. The merchants were called Chapmen, and their horses were naturally enough called Chapman Horses. Later on, they became known by the district of Cleveland from which they came. From this, plus the description of their bay color, which never varied, came the name Cleveland Bay.

During the late 1800's Thoroughbred blood was added to increase the size and give the horse more style (for it was a short, stubby little horse, as pack horses must be) and the Cleveland Bay became an all-purpose horse, used equally for driving, riding, and general farm work. The introduction of the hot blood was skillfully made, and a careful record, which had been kept since 1700, was continued, so that although the Cleveland Bay came to somewhat resemble the Thoroughbred, it still had the bay color only. A small white star is sometimes seen today, and occasionally there are white hairs in the coronet. Any further white marking is skeptically regarded as indicating outside blood. In the latter part of the nineteenth century, zebra stripes on the forearms and above the hocks were favorably looked upon. It was felt that they showed exceedingly pure breeding. Apparently, this was just a fad, for the markings are not seen today.

The Yorkshire Coach Horse is a close relative of the Cleveland Bay, and the two were even registered in the same stud book in the United States. With the advent of mechanization, however, the Yorkshire Coach Horse disappeared while the Cleveland Bay went on to other things. It was crossed with draft mares to produce a lightweight farm horse with good disposition and small feed requirements, and, as previously mentioned, it was used to produce heavyweight hunters. It was said that Cleveland Bay stallions and Thoroughbred mares produced better hunters than the reverse cross.

It is interesting to note that whereas there is very little call for the Cleveland Bay in America, in England the demand is greater than the supply, which speaks well for the survival of the Cleveland Bay in its native England if it cannot thrive here.

Clydesdale

Outstanding points of conformation:

HEIGHT AND WEIGHT: 16 to 17 hands, 1700 to 1900 pounds.

COLORS AND MARKINGS: most common are bay and brown, but black, gray, chestnut, and roan are sometimes found. White markings are extensive and almost always present on legs and face.

HEAD: broad between the eyes.

PROFILE: straight, or slightly convex.

NECK: long and well arched.

WITHERS: higher than most draft breeds.

MANE AND TAIL: tail is docked to about six inches, mane is often plaited in eight to twelve knobs.

FEATHER: the Clydesdale has the most feather of any draft breed except for the Shire, whose feather is coarser and thus heavier. It is very fine and silky and flows when the legs move.

No ONE WHO has seen a hitch of Clydesdales will ever forget them, those shiny big horses with flying white feet, and manes done up in a jaunty Aberdeen Roll. Most sightings are made at home through the medium of television, for manufacturers of such diverse items as meat, milk, and beer have discovered that the strikingly beautiful Clydesdale Horses can help to sell merchandise simply by pulling a wagonful of it across the television screen. It is mostly because of this magnetic appeal that the Clydesdale continues to be bred in America. It is also sometimes used at horse shows to pull loads of jump-rails and other paraphernalia used in the show ring, for this is a much more attractive and appropriate way to set up the arena than to use a truck.

The Clydesdale originated in Scotland near the River Clyde, from which it took its name. The Scotch were most interested in the legs and action of the Clydesdale, and beginning with a nondescript horse of uncertain origin (but probably a mixture of Flemish and English horses), they lavished upon it a great deal of care and attention until it became renowned for its beautiful action and excellent legs. They worked on the feather until it was fine, long, and flowing, and they concentrated on flashy white markings. It is a rare sight today to see a Clydesdale without considerable white on face and legs.

But despite their efforts on the legs and feet, they almost neglected the remaining conformation, so that the Clydesdale hasn't the weight and full muscle of the other breeds. It most nearly resembles the Shire, for the Shire, too, has abundant feather and rangy build, but the main differences are that the Clydesdale has a finer build, silkier feather, and more refinement.

By 1880, the Clydesdale was being imported to America in large numbers, chiefly to the northern parts of the United States and to Canada. It was used mainly in cities by merchants who desired a snappy, stylish mover with a good trot. The Clydesdale filled this order naturally, and soon was regarded as one of the better class of wagon horses.

Outside the cities, the Clydesdale found little favor. Unlike the Scotsman, the American farmer didn't care whether or not his workhorse had a brilliant walk and trot. He wasn't looking for style, but for usefulness and a coat easily kept neat. And in this

the Clydesdale failed in several respects, for in lifting its feet high it was wasting energy. Its long, fine feather quickly tangled with burrs and mud; its lovely white feet were immediately dirtied in the messy business of farming; and the white face was soon stained with sweat and dust. The farmer had the choice of cleaning up the mess at frequent intervals, letting them go to get worse and worse, or choosing a different kind of horse — and he usually chose another horse without white markings halfway up its legs and long tangly fetlock hair. Another disadvantage in the Clydesdale was its comparatively light weight. It simply did not have the bulk to throw against the collar to pull a heavy load. So the Clydesdale remained a city horse, to be later crowded out by trucks and buses.

The discovery of the Clydesdale by the advertising world changed the whole picture. Today it is a celebrity, and to perform its duties as a team member, each horse in a hitch has different things to learn. A hitch (or team) of horses is made of three sections: the lead horses, the wheel horses, and the swing horses. The lead horses are the pair at the head of the hitch. They must have quick action, for on turns they have the farthest to go. The wheel horses are the pair closest to the wagon, and their job is the hardest, for they do most of the pulling on turns, so they are chosen for their strength and endurance. The horses paired up between the lead and wheel pairs must be fast on their feet, for through the center of the swing pair or pairs passes the swinging pole or tongue of the wagon, and if they do not stay out of its way they will be thoroughly thumped and will slow the movement of the wagon.

Despite the shortcomings of the Clydesdale, the Scotsman has always used it in agriculture. Perhaps it is his pride in his animals and his vanity about their beauty that has made him willing to unsnarl the fine feather and wash muddy legs. Although it is still used some in Scotland, the breed is now mostly produced and used in Ireland where the majority of farming is still done in elegant style by the lofty Clydesdale Draft Horse.

Cream Draft

Outstanding points of conformation:

HEIGHT AND WEIGHT: 15 to 17 hands; 1700 to 2000 pounds.

COLORS AND MARKINGS: since this is a color breed in part, only cream color is admitted, with white mane and tail. White markings are usual. Eyes are amber.

GENERAL CONFORMATION: the Cream Draft has no particular points of conformation other than color. It is a good average draft horse, of medium-heavy weight.

MANE AND TAIL: the mane and tail are left free and flowing. The tail is not docked.

FEATHER: slight, about as much as the Percheron's.

IT MAY SEEM odd, in this age of mechanization, that any group might be trying to organize and promote a new breed of draft horses. It is true that the real need for the draft horse is gone. Tractors are generally more efficient, can work longer and harder hours, and needn't take time off to bear and nurse young. They don't have to be fed morning and night, nor cleaned up after. Admittedly, there are advantages in the tractor.

But there are some advantages it doesn't have, as well. A horse can replace itself nearly free of charge through its foals, although it causes a few delays in work. It costs less in hard cash to make a horse run efficiently than to keep a tractor gassed, oiled, and overhauled, and the tractor doesn't produce fertilizer as a by-product. The farmer needn't climb up and down from the machine for the sole purpose of advancing it a few feet — a "giddap" or

"whoa" will put the team just where he needs it with no effort on his part. And there is something else, too. A tractor can't nuzzle your shoulder in thanks for a measure of grain or a stop for water, and there is nothing quite like the sight of a big horse shaking itself when the harness comes off then trotting out into the green grass of the pasture for a good roll.

All these things: the cost, the companionship, the ease of long-distance handling, and many intangibles that are difficult to count in terms of work, have caused the people who know and love the American Cream Draft Horse to present it to the American people for consideration.

Of all the draft breeds, the Cream Draft is the only American model. It was initiated in the early 1900's by a well-built cream-colored draft mare of unknown breeding, named Old Granny. All her get bore her distinctive looks and color. With her, the breed began. And with the judicious addition of the blood of excellent specimens from the Percheron, Shire, and Belgian breeds, a distinct type was formed. Uniform in color and conformation, the Cream Draft cuts a unique figure. Other draft breeds seldom, if ever, turn up a cream-colored animal, so the Cream Drafts draw the attention of all who see them. Unfortunately, they have always been limited to a small area in the Midwest. Perhaps the future will see their dispersion over the country.

The American Cream Draft Horse Association was formed in 1944 to record the pedigrees which had been kept informally up to that point, set up a constructive breeding program to confirm the bloodlines, and determine goals and requirements. The American Cream they evolved is a striking animal of medium draft weight. Its color is a uniform medium cream, which makes it simple to form matching teams either for the farmer's viewing pleasure while he works, or for use in parades and shows.

To get the proper shade of cream each time, only horses with pink skins are used, for dark-skinned creams have changeable coat colors. The eyes are amber, an unusual color and a shade peculiar to the American Cream. The young foal's eyes are almost white, but as the animal matures they gradually darken until a deep honey color is reached. The mane and tail are white, and some white markings on the face and legs are encouraged, for they present a pleasant contrast against the rich creamy coat.

The American Cream is singular in the fact that its tail is never docked. The purpose of docking, as explained by people who use docked draft animals, is to keep the tail out of the way of the traces (which connect the load to the horse's harness) and to prevent its being caught in machinery. But docking isn't really necessary if due precautions are taken, and although it is neater, a docked tail keeps the horse from protecting itself from biting flies. And a horse that must fight flies without the use of its tail can be an irritable animal indeed.

The call for draft horses will probably always be limited, for most farmers choose the efficiency of the tractor over the joys of working with a team. But there will always be farmers who like to stay close to the land and savor the warmth of the sun and feel the worn leather of the reins from a seat behind the broad rump of a draft horse. To these men, the Cream Draft belongs.

Percheron

Outstanding points of conformation:

HEIGHT AND WEIGHT: 16 to 17 hands; 1900 to 2000 pounds.

COLORS AND MARKINGS: about 90 percent of Percherons are black or gray. The rest are roan, sorrel, or bay. White markings are somewhat limited; on a gray horse the white on the face may be just a lighter shade of gray.

FACE: is the most refined of the draft breeds, being straight or slightly convex, but sometimes very slightly dished.

BODY: is lighter than the Belgian, but more compact and sturdy than the Clydesdale or Shire. About the same as the Suffolk.

MANE AND TAIL: tail is usually docked, although sometimes not.

FEATHER: very little, much less than Clydesdale and Shire, but more than the Belgian.

THE MOST POPULAR heavy draft horse at the beginning of this century was the hearty, bold Percheron. Because of its adaptability and early start in America (in the 1830's), it outnumbered all the other draft breeds combined. The Percheron was a favorite for crossing on grade mares, and their get was usually dapple-gray or black and always brought the highest prices at the auction block.

The nicest thing about the Percheron was that it was a jack-of-all-trades. Lighter and rangier than the Belgian, it showed more speed and action, making it a vastly superior carriage and cross-country wagon horse. It was heavier and stronger than the Clydesdale, able to pull a big load farther, with nearly as much style. The Shire and Suffolk Punch were so rare as to offer hardly any competition, so most farmers turned gladly to the Percheron.

Strangely enough, the Percheron didn't start out to be a heavy draft horse, and was used regularly as a saddle horse until the 1820's. In the Middle Ages in France, it was sometimes used as a charger by knights, so it must have had quite a bit of substance and soundness, but the French have always been more interested in style than their neighboring countrymen. While the Belgian horses got heavier and coarser, the French were introducing Arab blood to their heavy horses. The result was a handsome general purpose horse of 15 or 16 hands, and it was used as a saddle horse, hunter, and carriage horse. Some sires were recorded as being Turkish horses, others were Thoroughbred type, while Arabian blood was introduced periodically between A.D. 735 and 1820, at which time the Percheron was put to use in France pulling omnibuses. The Percheron's color was always gray for visibility at night, the color coming from Arabian blood. Dapple-gray and black are about the only colors seen today, although sometimes sorrel appears.

When first imported to the United States, the Percheron was called the Norman Horse. This was later changed to Percheron to distinguish the horse bred in Le Perche, France, from the several other draft breeds from other parts of France, who were also called Norman Horses. The first American Stud Book was published in 1876, and the Percheron Horse Association of America was established in 1905 under the name of Percheron Society of America. By 1965, nearly a quarter of a million Percherons had been registered.

The 1880's showed the greatest number of importations of the Norman Horse and by this time the pioneers were settling the West. Naturally they took their finest and strongest workhorses, the Percherons far outnumbering any other type. The Percheron was perfectly adapted both to the long westward trek and for all kinds of work after reaching the destination. For some reason, most Percheron owners settled in the Northwest (possibly because it was the best farming land), and this had an unprecedented effect on the northern mustang herds.

There were no fences then, and the wild herds ran off with many Percheron mares, with the result that there began to appear dapple-grays among the wild ones. Eventually, many of the northern herds had a majority of heavily built dappled horses, but the usual outcome of breeding mustang to Percheron was poor, for the offspring tended to be an ungainly and ugly lot. Some crosses were made intentionally by farmers to create an all-purpose horse, but the results seldom warranted the effort. People who had an opportunity to ride them derisively called them Puddingfoots, while a similar cross of Clydesdales on mustangs in Oregon acquired the name of Oregon Lummox.

While the Percheron was about the last to feel the pinch of automation because of its remote position in the western states, it also swiftly declined in numbers after the appearance of tractors. There was and is one place where the Percheron maintains a foothold, and that is with the Amish people, often called Pennsylvania Dutch, who disdain the use of machinery. Percherons are still to be found in some backwoods logging ventures, too, and on small midwest and northwestern farms. Percherons are featured in big parade hitches as well, a glorious sight with their bright dappled coats. The light coloring has also given them another niche, for they are used almost exclusively by circus bareback riders because the white rosin smeared on their broad backs does not show against the gray and white hairs.

The future for the Percheron is limited but quite hopeful. Registrations have increased steadily for the last few years, and it looks as though the faithful Percheron is here to stay.

Shire

Outstanding points of conformation:

HEIGHT AND WEIGHT: 16 to 18 hands; 2000 or more pounds.
COLORS AND MARKINGS: black, bay, brown, roan, and gray. White stockings usual,
                     also white markings on face.
PROFILE: nearly always roman-nosed.
EARS: long and sharp.
HEAD: lean.
PASTERNS: are much shorter than Clydesdale's.
MANE AND TAIL: hair is coarse and kinky.
FEATHER: long and thick, kinky and coarse. The most voluminous of all the breeds.

AN 18-HAND HORSE stands six feet tall at the top of its withers. With its head in a normally alert position, it would probably be about seven and one half feet from the ground to the top of its head (the average ceiling in a house is eight feet high). This is the size of a large Shire Draft Horse.

The huge size, averaging between 16 and 18 hands, is the hallmark of the Shire. So, too, are its great weight and sluggish temperament, but along with the sluggishness comes an amiable nature that makes the Shire a pleasant horse to work with, since it doesn't require special or experienced handling.

The American farmer, as a rule, preferred the Belgian and the Percheron to the Shire, and when draft horses were at their peak numbers, the Shire held the third position in United States popularity. Some of the farmers' objections were about its lack of alertness and the very sluggishness that made it an easy worker,

for the farmer generally needed a horse with more all-around utility than the Shire could manage. Since it was so big and heavy, it was perfect for pulling large loads, but it was difficult for it to do a light job swiftly, and it simply could not do it with any sort of style or refinement.

The cities, on the other hand, were very pleased with the Shire. They found it to be perfect for the heaviest sort of hauling, for with its great mass it did not have to resort to jerking and heaving to get the cart started, but could merely lean slowly into the collar with immediate results.

While any other horse would soon be exhausted or was too spirited for such dull, heavy work, the Shire was dependable and contented.

The Shire was somewhat popular on the open ranges of the West for producing crossbreds. If size and quality were desired in a crossbred, the Shire was the most likely of all the draft breeds to produce good results. In addition, heavily feathered legs appeared on the offspring, proving their sire was a Shire. This was particularly important with open range horses, for otherwise the draft breeding could not be verified.

At one time, the Shire was profusely haired, not only on the back of its legs in the form of feather, but also having a little tuft of hair sprouting from the front of each knee and from the point of each hock. Furthermore, the Shire sported a mustache on its lower lip. This hairiness was felt to denote particular purity, but American buyers didn't like it, and it fell from general favor and was bred out.

The history of the Shire is much the same as the other European draft breeds. It descended from the same Horse of Flanders or Flemish Horse that was the ancestor of the Clydesdale and Belgian. It was a crossing of Great Horse and Roman Horse, designed first for carrying knights, then for agriculture and carting. The roads built by the Romans directly encouraged the formation of the draft breeds in Britain and Europe, for with roads the drafter could be used to pull big wagons and coaches, thus materially aiding the prosperity of the communities. But the differences between the Shire, Belgian, and Clydesdale Horses can only be explained by the variations in the aims and ideals of the breeders in the different countries. Except for large size, the Shire is not very similar to the otherwise closely related Clydesdale, having heavier bone and little style or refinement.

The Shire had many different names throughout its history. It was known as the Great Horse, the War Horse, the Cart Horse, the Giant Lincolnshire, and the Old English Black Horse. One name in general favor, from the time of Oliver Cromwell on, was Large Black Old English Horse — quite a burdensome name to bestow on any creature. The English Cart Horse Society was formed in 1878 to promote the breed, and it later changed its name to the Shire Horse Society. The American Shire Horse Association was formed in 1885.

Although there are a few Shires left in America, there has been a recent move to revitalize the breed by individual breeders, who, for their own pleasure, would like to see the Shire Horse once again commonplace in America. There is no such problem in Britain, for there the Shire is numerous and well loved. It helps to farm the shires (counties) and fens (marshes), where tractors are neither usable nor economical, and those who love draft horses and all they stand for can only hope the situation stays that way.

Suffolk Punch

Outstanding points of conformation:

HEIGHT AND WEIGHT: 16 to 17:1 hands; 1800 to 2300 pounds.
COLORS AND MARKINGS: the only color allowed is chestnut, with the mane and tail frequently flaxen or cream. White markings are seldom seen, sometimes a white snip or a coronet.
HEAD: is long, bony, large for size of horse, but handsome.
EARS: small.
LEGS: are short, making the body seem longer than it is.
RIBS: have pronounced spring, making body quite round.
CROUP: is the straightest of all draft breeds, sloping croups seldom seen on Suffolks.
MANE AND TAIL: average, tail is generally docked.

THERE MIGHT STILL be some Suffolk Punch Horses in the United States, although probably very few by now, for registrations of the Suffolk have nearly stopped in America. Still, it would not be right to discuss all the other draft breeds that contributed to the cultivation of rural America and leave out the Suffolk Punch.

The Suffolk Punch was a fine little drafter, standing shorter than any of the other draft breeds, with a smooth rotund body and invariably a chestnut coat. The chestnut coloring came in all hues, including dark and bright red, yellow, gold, copper, and liver, and it was sometimes set off by a tiny white star on the face or snip on the heel. The uniform coloring is credited to the founder of the breed, the Crisp Horse, which lived in Suffolk County, eastern England, in 1768. The short legs are said to have come from a

short-legged trotting stallion introduced to the breed in 1773 to improve the Suffolk's looks and action. To add size to the breed, a large chestnut stallion contributed its blood in the early 1800's. Since that time, all breeding has been pure, the purest of any of the draft breeds, every horse tracing back to the Crisp Horse. The Suffolk Punch is the drafter best loved in England for its easy keeping, persistence at the collar, and cheery disposition.

Cart pulling and road hauling were not what the Suffolk was designed for, although it was used for a time to pull England's earliest road coaches. While other breeds were used for both road and farm, the Suffolk remained contentedly on England's farms and shires, doing what it was bred for.

In the late 1800's when America was looking for draft breeds to import, England was very possessive with its Suffolk Punch. It was loathe to part with its finest stock or any other kind, either, since the farms only produced about what they needed for their own use. But a few were finally acquired by persistent American buyers, and importing gradually increased as the demand grew and English farmers began to breed a few extra Suffolks for export.

The Suffolk Punch was appreciated in America where it became known, but the breed's growth and spread were exceedingly slow because of the small number of purebred stock available. The American farmers discovered, to their great pleasure, that the Suffolk could do a larger share of labor for a longer time and with smaller food requirements than the other draft breeds. It is very likely that the Suffolk Punch would have posed a very serious threat to the dominance of the Percheron if all draft breeds hadn't been put out of business by motorized machinery.

With its big round barrel from which it took its name "punch" (Some say it means the horse looked "punched up" or "punchy," and others say the word came from "paunch," both of which are possible and equally descriptive, for the breed was once known for its excessive pottiness, to which American farmers objected. This, plus defective feet and legs were successfully bred out of the breed) and its short legs, it could throw itself into the harness down on a level with the load for a direct pull with excellent results. It had several advantages over the Percheron in other maters, too, for its chestnut coat was easier to keep clean than the gray-turning-white hair of the Percheron, it had even less fetlock hair than the Percheron to get muddied and tangled, and it was an easier keeper than any other draft breed. In addition, it was able, because of its compactness, to keep a balanced conformation even if it became thin from poor feed.

Suffolks were to be found in America mostly in Iowa, Washington, Oregon, and some eastern states, in which they were beginning to gain quite a bit of popularity by 1900.

Although the Suffolk has nearly disappeared in America, it is still to be found in limited numbers in its native England. It has been used with some success in breeding heavyweight hunters and riding horses, but as with any match of hot and cold blood, the results are not always predictable.

Fecundity and longevity are two of the Suffolk's finest points.

It isn't uncommon for a farmer to get a foal every year from his Suffolk mare, working her all the while except for a couple of weeks around foaling time. And she might still be producing at thirty-seven, as one mare on record did. It is a real shame that the Suffolk had no chance to take its rightful place beside the other draft breeds in America.

DONKEY, JACK, and MULE

American Jack

Ideal conformation:

HEIGHT AND WEIGHT: 15:2 to 16 hands; 1075 to 1200 pounds.
COLORS AND MARKINGS: most popular is black with white nose, white ring around the eye, white underline, and white on insides of legs. Red jacks are fairly common, but gray is disliked.
HEAD: is carried erect, is somewhat large.
EARS: may measure thirty-three inches from tip to tip when horizontal.
EYES: large and alert.
FACE: straight or roman-nosed. Straight is considered better.
CHEST: wide and deep, well muscled.
FOREARM: heavily muscled.
SHOULDER: well sloped.
JOINTS: large and flat.
HOOVES, FORE AND REAR: deep, round, large, and durable.
RIBS: well sprung.
TOP LINE: straight and long.
COUPLING: short and heavy.
CROUP: long, well muscled.
HIPS: smooth muscling.
GASKIN: heavily muscled.
SKIN: the skin is considerably thicker over the back and shoulders than in horses.
MANE AND TAIL: short mane is often roached.

THE AMERICAN JACK seems to be fading from the American scene, or at best barely holding its own. It has a unique place in the equine world in that it was never meant for working or as a show animal but was intended only for breeding. It was evolved and

perfected on the southern plantations and farms to produce mules for the various plantation tasks of hauling, plowing, and cultivating the land, and sometimes to produce riding mules. This was the day of the American Jack, when its breeding was lucrative big business with an unceasing demand for mules and more mules.

When the mule breeders had caught up with the demands of the farming South, the Civil War and later World War I used up any excess, and the government bought at good prices all that they could provide. But the tractor and motorized war vehicles ended all that. Now, with the need for mules at a bare minimum, there is little call for the big, standardized, black Jacks that created them; little reason to mate them to sturdy mares for the production of hardy, horse-sized mules.

The American Jack has a distinguished history in America. Before the Revolutionary War, there were no Jacks whatever in this country. Their export was forbidden from Spain by its royal rulers, so mules were not available to the Americans. In 1787, in a moment of friendly benevolence, the king of Spain, having heard of General George Washington's interest in attempting to raise mules, sent him a royal gift of a gray Andalusian Jack and Jennet. From General Lafayette, Washington received a Maltese Jack and several Jennets. And from these two breeds sprang the nucleus of the American Jack. Another prominent breeder and importer, once the restriction had been lifted, was Henry Clay of Kentucky, who imported Maltese stock in 1827. During the next

sixty years, importing included all the European breeds, and totaled high in the thousands. France has a huge donkey called the Poitou which stands 15 to 16 hands and has long matted hair, giving it a decidedly scruffy appearance. However, its conformation is drafty to the ideal and one was introduced in this country in the late 1930's to provide some much needed blood for outcrossing.

The American Jack of today is pretty much of a composite, but its conformation is uniform from one animal to the next. Some of the most prevalent blood is Catalonian, from which it gets the usual black coloring with white points, and Andalusian, which is stylish and handsome, but gray. In the beginning of the breed, the Andalusian blood was more predominant, but the gray coat, turning white with age, was transmitted to its mule progeny, and farmers hesitated to buy a mule which would show the dirt so obviously when they could have a different color if they wanted.

A good Jack has conformation much like that of the draft horse. Its joints and bones are large, and it has small round feet. The head isn't usually especially handsome, but then, *Equus asinus* isn't known for its beautiful facial features. The jack must stand 14 hands or more, have a girth of at least sixty inches, and a forecannon circumference of seven and a half inches at the minimum. Jennies should attain a minimum of 13:2 hands and seven-inch forecannon circumference. The emphasis on the heavy forecannons stems from the fact that the animal will usually have good bones if the cannons are sturdy. Like all donkeys, the American Jack is quite long-lived, thirty-five and forty-year-old individuals being not too uncommon.

The principle difference between an American Jack and an ordinary, unlettered donkey, ass, or burro is its pedigree. Generally speaking, an ordinary donkey doesn't grow to 14 hands, either. Most run-of-the-mill donkeys have rather nondescript conformation, since they aren't often bred with an eye to form but left to propagate as they will. The difference between donkey and burro seems to be one of location — a western donkey is a burro, and an eastern burro is a donkey. The word "ass," unfortunately, has acquired an unsavory meaning and is seldom used in polite company.

Burro or Donkey

Ideal conformation:

HEIGHT: 8 to 15 hands.

COLORS AND MARKINGS: most common color is gray with white belly, nose, legs, and spectacles. Other colors run through white, cream, tan, brown, and even black with tan points. Pinto markings are rarely seen. Black shoulder cross and eel stripe are always present; stripes on legs are common.

HEAD: large in proportion to body.

EARS: each at least nine inches long, often more than a foot.

PROFILE: is usually roman-nosed.

WITHERS: usually very low.

LEGS: short and often spindly looking, but very strong.

HOOVES, FORE AND REAR: small and narrow, the rear feet smaller than the front.

BODY: long and narrow, sometimes potty.

CHESTNUTS: none on back legs.

MANE AND TAIL: mane is sparse and short with no forelock. Tail is short-haired except for tuft at end.

JENNY: is usually smaller than jack; is not as fertile as females of most other species; has a twelve-month gestation period as compared to the horse's eleven-month gestation period.

THE MINING INDUSTRY in the West would never have gotten off the ground had it not been for the strong, nimble burro. It was the faithful companion and burden-bearer for the prospector (who often adopted it as his family and slept and ate with it), and when the precious ores were discovered and men had no other way to haul in supplies and tunnel timbers, the little sure-footed burros

Burro and Burro Foal

carried on where no horses could travel, much less pack! There are probably as many burros now as there ever were. Prospectors still use them — although the prospector is just as likely to be a college student with a Geiger counter as a bearded old codger.

Burros tote tourists up and down mountain trails on dude ranches during the summer months, and hunters and hikers trust them with their camping gear as they take to the mountains in search of game or adventure. Children find them excellent companions on the trail, for when the youngster tires of walking he can shinny up onto a firm (if sharp) little back and take an upper view for a while. On the whole, there isn't a more delightful or helpful companion on the trail, for although the burro sets its feet firmly if you face it and tug, it will follow quietly if you simply walk away.

It isn't really surprising that the burro has a reputation for stubbornness, but it should be kept in mind that most people don't realize its limitations. Too often, people have loaded it with a heavier pack than a horse could carry, then wonder why it won't budge. It will balk too, if the pack starts to slip (while a horse will panic and bolt), and it most certainly does have a mind of its own; but patience and understanding can usually solve the problem, and a well-treated burro is almost never willfully stubborn.

Burro is the name given to the small donkey found in the West and Southwest, but just where the division comes between donkey and burro is debatable. There is no registry for ordinary donkeys and burros, although there is one for miniature donkeys.

Burros (or donkeys, whichever you prefer) have a long and interesting history. They were first domesticated for pack and draft animals along the Nile River in Egypt, the jennies often being used for riding animals. These donkeys, which descended from wild asses of Africa, and other wild asses from Asia were taken into Europe, where they branched out into the different types found there today. Most of the original stock is gone now, and has been extinct since Roman times. Unlike the horse's, the donkey's appearance has scarcely changed through the ages.

The main duties of the donkey in its homeland are to pull plows and thresh wheat, to turn millstones, and to work in mines.

Although it has always been a beast of burden, the ass was not at first despised. It was highly valued, in fact, and high prices were often paid for good animals. Throughout the centuries, however, it came more and more to be the property and transportation of the peasant and poor man, for its ability to exist on thistles and straw if necessary made it the only animal that the commoner could afford to feed. Because of its association with the poor and low-caste people it came to be looked down upon by proud and haughty upper classes.

The noise it makes, commonly called a bray, certainly doesn't add glamour to its image. It starts with a wheeze and a whistle, with maybe a snort or two, and after the engine charges up for several seconds, there is a sound like the opening of a large door with rusty hinges. All of which might send the listener hastening off to find an oil can, except that it is obviously the burro making all the noise, showing the whole underside of its upper lip, its eyes closed, its nose pointing skyward, tail revolving slowly, and every one of its teeth showing — without any doubt ecstatically enjoying every creaking gasp.

Mule

Ideal conformation:

HEIGHT: 12 to 17:2 hands.

COLORS AND MARKINGS: may have all colors and markings that horses are known to have.

GENERAL CONFORMATION: head, ears, feet, and bone are similar to the donkey's. Body and legs are like the horse's, and muscling is midway between the donkey's and the horse's. There are no chestnuts on the hind legs.

MANE AND TAIL: mane is donkey-like, tail is horselike but sparse. Since the mule is a hybrid and cannot produce offspring (each animal is the product of a donkey and horse), little attention is paid to its conformation as long as it can perform successfully. Therefore, there are standards for horses and donkeys destined for mule production, but none for mule conformation itself.

A NEWS BROADCAST in the spring of 1967 had an item that came as quite a shock to most people who heard it, for it was naturally assumed that the mule was dropped from all military service after World War I. The broadcast reported that mules were being used daily by the British around the perimeter of Hong Kong to haul guns to areas inaccessible to jeeps and helicopters, that they helped patrol the border around the city, and that Americans were also considering using them in similar circumstances.

It isn't really surprising that the mule continues to demonstrate its great versatility and usefulness, for there has never been a more useful animal in the service of man than the mule. It can

work harder and longer than any horse, with less food and water, and in extreme hot or cold temperatures. It will not founder itself by overeating as horses have been known to do, and it will not allow itself to be overworked (to the chagrin of many a frustrated mule driver).

In the same general class as the mule is the hinny. While a mule is produced by crossing a jack stallion with a mare, a hinny is the result of a horse stallion and a jenny. Few hinnies are to be found for two reasons: stallions are very reluctant to interbreed with a jenny, and any jenny that would produce a fine hinny is usually saved for producing fine donkeys instead. Hinnies are different from mules in several respects, although cursory examination might overlook the fine points. The hinny has more the disposition of its horse parent and less of its mother's stubbornness. Its head is more horselike, and its feet are round instead of U-shaped. Ancient Chinese and Persians prized the hinny as a riding mount. Hinnies and mules are nearly always infertile, but there are a few rare cases on record in which a mare mule conceived and produced a foal with only horse characteristics.

The mule has been in America since colonial times and the advent of mule breeding by George Washington. The Spaniards had them in 1591, but of course they never proliferated since they are sterile. Early mules were usually a cross of Maltese and Andalusian jack on native horses, the mare determining the size and type of mule. In time, there came to be four types of mules.

The sugar and cotton mules were large and rangy, with good quality, being used on the sugar and cotton plantations in the South. Similar mules of that same general type are still used in the South today by sharecroppers. Draft mules stood up to 17 hands, had draft-horse build, and were used for hauling purposes, road repair and building, railroad building, and lumbering, sometimes working in long hitches of twenty or more mules. Farm mules were a miscellaneous lot, used for any farming task at hand. And the mining mules came in large and small sizes, large jacks being used for surface mining, and small jacks, the result of burro-pony breeding, were used in the pits and tunnels.

The Americans were one of the greatest mule users of all time, except perhaps for ancient Romans who used them extensively for war and the imperial postal service. The West was won and kept with the mule, and when the American soldier went to war, the mule went with him. Five thousand mules perished on the battle-fields of World War I alone, and they were praised for their usefulness in all aspects of war. The mule was found to be impervious to many horse diseases, was only half as susceptible to shipping fever, and never had to take time out to foal.

Mules are not nearly so common as they once were, not being necessary in great numbers for war and agriculture. There are some people who claim that the mule is the perfect riding mount, and they set up a registry called the International Mule Association in 1964. Otherwise, the mule is mostly used for packing in the wilderness areas by hunters, hikers, and tourists. In some rough mountain areas, it is used for logging. Anyone who uses mules must be aware of the proper way to handle them. One soon learns that, as with the donkey, it does little good to tug at the halter, but if he walks off in the direction he wants it to go, pulling gently, the mule will follow. A courteously handled mule will usually react in a mannerly fashion.

The average mule today is of medium size, about 15 hands, for easy packing and handling. Its back is short and straight, its legs strong, and it is an agile trail animal. If a packer has a number of identical mules, he may use the time-honored system of identification by "belling" the tail. He clips out a hunk of tail to form each bell, and finding "Ol' Three-bell Tom" in the early morning mist is an easy task for even the greenest dude.

WILD EQUINES

Burchell's Zebra

LIKE NORTH AMERICA'S great shaggy bison, Africa's zebras once roamed their native plains and mountains in limitless numbers. Their predators were sufficient — lions took their usual toll and occasionally a zebra fell prey to a hyena, cape hunting dog, or some other hungry animal. The balance of nature took care of itself as it always does when left undisturbed. And then, like the bison, the zebras came to the attention of the white man, who, true to form, began a mindless slaughter which decimated Africa's great striped herds until some races, the Quagga, for one, met untimely and needless extinction.

While there have been some more or less successful efforts at conservation, the fate of Africa's wild equines now hangs on the balance of an uneasy world situation in which it may become more important to accommodate a rapidly increasing human population than to protect future zebra numbers.

At present, however, the zebras are fairly well protected, and there are three species, each of which warrants examination: Burchell's Zebra, the Mountain Zebra, and Grévy's Zebra.

Burchell's Zebra, named after the British explorer and naturalist, is the most common zebra to be found and is also the species about which the most confusion revolves. It is variously called the Common Zebra, Grant's Zebra, Chapman's Zebra, Quagga, and Bontequagga, as well as Burchell's Zebra. In addition, there is carelessness about its scientific name, both *Equus burchelli* and *Equus quagga* being used. To be accurate, *burchelli* is just a subspecies (as are *grantii* and *chapmanii*) and is only properly added to the end, as in *Equus quagga burchelli*, *Equus*

quagga grantii, etc. The confusion about Quagga and Bontequagga is interesting. The word "Quagga" came from the Boer Dutch of Africa, and referred to the barking cry, a plaintive "kway-hay" of the zebras native to that region. The most common zebra there was only half-striped, and it became known as the Quagga. It was a beautiful animal with the scientific name of *Equus quagga quagga* and had dark stripes on a fawn or chestnut background covering the head, neck, shoulders, and part of the barrel. But midway back on the barrel, the stripes stopped, and the hind part of the body was solid color, while the legs and belly were cream or white. The Boers' name for the fully striped Burchell's Zebra, Bontequagga, simply meant "brightly striped Quagga." But the Quagga was doomed to extinction, for the Boer farmers killed staggering numbers of them to feed their Hottentot laborers, and by the mid-1870's there were none left. It is difficult to obtain accurate information about the Quagga because of the confusion that occurred between the two terms, Quagga and Bontequagga. Burchell's Zebra was formerly found from central Africa to the Cape Colony on the southern tip of the continent. It still exists in large numbers in the northern end of the range, but in the southern end, where it was partly represented by the Quagga, it is much more scarce.

Burchell's Zebra is pony size, standing about 12 hands, sometimes more. It is lighter boned than any of the other zebras, with a fine supple neck and nicely formed legs. Its extremely low withers give the false impression of a very long back. The barrel of Burchell's Zebra is well rounded, and in the wild it usually presents a potty appearance due to its heavy grass diet; in captivity, all zebras have smaller bellies. Its head is fairly heavy and blunt when viewed from the side, and the ears are early horse size. The tail is tufted at the end, like a donkey's.

Quagga

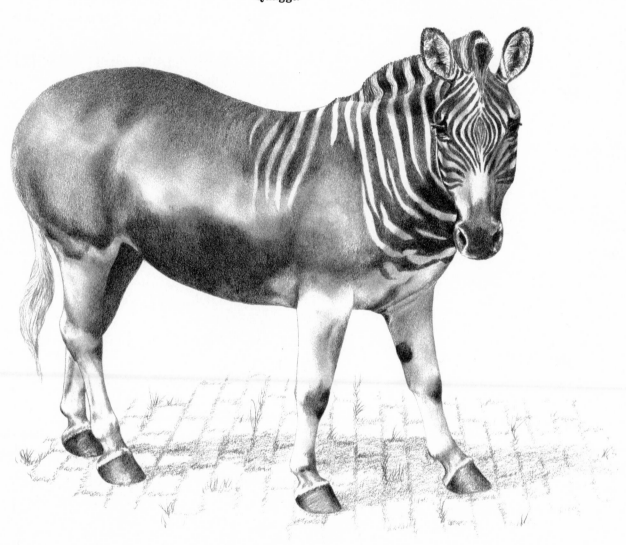

The base color of the coat ranges from buff to white, and the stripes may be any shade from dark brown to black and are sometimes alternated with shadow stripes (paler stripes). The stripes are broad over the entire body, extending in most animals down to the coronet. Toward the central and southern part of the African continent, however, the stripes tend to be faded or missing on the legs and underline. In contrast, some Burchell's Zebras are so strongly shadow-striped as to be almost solidly marked black and brown. The pattern of the stripes is slanting on the croup, vertical on the front half of the body, and horizontal on the legs. The wide stripes of the croup extend across the flank and meet the vertical stripes at the center of the barrel, making a large V. While these markings are extremely conspicuous in a zoo or green pasture, they effectively break up the zebra's outline on the stark, tree-dotted veldts of Africa, making it almost invisible at a distance (especially when it is resting under a scrub tree during a hot afternoon) both day and night.

No two zebras are marked exactly alike, although the general species pattern is followed. The stripes are so random that both sides of the same zebra aren't even alike.

Burchell's Zebra is a speedy animal, able to sustain thirty-five miles per hour for a long distance, the initial burst of speed being even faster. Since it is the most common zebra, *Equus quagga burchelli* has been the most thoroughly studied of all the zebra species. The mode of living is quite similar to that of the American mustangs in earlier days. They roam in herds composed of about fifteen mares and foals, and one stallion. The young males leave when they are one to three years old and join bachelor herds until they are strong and old enough to get and hold a harem of their own. The competition for herds is strong and requires constant vigilance, since the only ways to begin a harem are to either steal a complete herd from an old stallion (a long, tough battle) or to abduct a filly. Breeding takes place the year around, but more than three-fourths of the births occur between October and April, summertime in the Southern Hemisphere. The average life span is fifteen years.

Because of its numbers and availability, Burchell's Zebra has come under man's influence and has been broken to harness with fair results. It was common opinion in those days that since the Burchell's Zebra was comparatively easy to break in and would breed in confinement, it would soon become a domesticated animal. Since it had little or no tendency to contract what was then called "horse sickness" from the deadly tsetse fly, it would have been a valuable draft and riding animal. Had not motorized vehicles appeared on the scene, Africa very likely would have been second to none in flashy draft "horses."

Around the beginning of the century, the larger circuses had Burchell's Zebra performing in liberty acts with no restraining devices but bridles and sometimes fancy girth straps. Some acts featured them jumping through hoops and rolling barrels, and they were often harnessed to floats and carts in the big circus street parades. Perhaps it was inexpert handling, but then again, there may be some measure of truth in the general consensus at the time that their performance was poor: that they required constant vigilance, were stubborn, untrustworthy, and tired quickly. Perhaps trainers would have had better luck with the Quagga, for it was reputed to be strong and heavily built, although comparatively slower than Burchell's Zebra, and some authorities of the day reported that it should have been suitable for breaking to both harness and saddle with good results.

Burchell's Zebra

Grévy's Zebra

THERE IS some dispute about whether or not Grévy's Zebra belongs in the genus *Equus* with the horses, asses, hemiones, and the other zebras. Some authorities, on the basis of anatomical differences, place it alone in a new genus with the name *Doliochippus grevyi*. Others argue that the divergence is only superficial, and that it should be called *Equus grevyi*. Whatever the case, it is merely a matter of degree, and the name *Equus grevyi* seems to be the more widely accepted of the two (although the other will be found on occasion — they are both the same animal). At least there is no argument about its common name, and Grévy's Zebra is always Grévy's Zebra. It is the largest of all the zebras, averaging 13:2 hands and sometimes reaching as much as 14 hands, about the size of a small Quarter Horse or Arabian.

It is easily distinguished from the other zebras by the closely spaced narrow black stripes covering its entire body except for a broad white area flanking the black median line on its rump, and a white belly. The stripes on the head and neck are quite a bit wider than those on the body, and the stripes on the croup are vertical and slim instead of horizontal and wide like those of the other zebras. Grévy's Zebra has a long, dolorous face, the expression heightened by the vertical stripes stretching its length to a velvety black nose. Despite its length, the head is well proportioned, and the huge, rounded, donkey-like ears do not look out of place. Without the stripes, large ears, and tufted tail, it might easily be taken for a horse due to its conformation and horselike neigh. In view of this, it is somewhat surprising to observe that Grévy's Zebra seems to have seldom, if ever, been engaged by man in his endless pursuit of taming and mastering *Equus* for draft and riding. Perhaps its shy and retiring nature makes it difficult to approach and pacify. It lives in semiarid thornbush country of Kenya, Ethiopia, and Somalia in East Africa. For mutual protection the Grévy's Zebra often joins forces with bands of Beisa Oryx, a rapier-horned antelope with vivid black face and forearm markings. This alliance evidently gives pause to lions, who are their chief enemies.

The most abundant food to be found in the range of this zebra is not grass but browse, and it has adapted admirably, living on twigs and leaves and going for days without drinking when driven away from water. The Grévy's Zebra is territorial, stallions claiming a particular piece of ground and defending it against all comers. This isn't an infallible rule, however, for sometimes mixed herds are found with a complement of more than one adult male.

Habits of the various species and even subspecies vary from one zebra to the next, but their common ancestry is shown quite clearly in the ability to interbreed between species and produce living young, even though the result is generally sterile. While the different species of zebra vary and intergrade to such an extent that it is sometimes difficult to tell where one ends and another starts, the zebras themselves never make this mistake and will not interbreed except when encouraged in captivity.

Mountain Zebra

THE MOUNTAIN ZEBRA, *Equus zebra*, is one of the so-called untamable zebras. Granted, it is the wildest of the three species, but it is definitely trainable and has been broken to ride successfully. There were numerous reports of its having been used in harness around the end of the last century. One of the difficulties encountered is its strong, thick neck, for it is a struggle to teach this zebra to turn since its neck is not flexible and it can bull its way through any turn signal if it desires. If trained early enough, however, less difficulty would be encountered than in trying to teach a grown specimen.

The Mountain Zebra is a pretty animal, and it would probably have become a more common riding animal had not the horseless carriage come along at the precise time that Africa was starting to feel the need for more speedy conveyances than the oxcarts. It is a shame that this colorful zebra missed that chance. Had it become domesticated, its continued existence might be better assured than it presently is, for it is nearly on the edge of extinction.

Smallest of all the zebras, the Mountain Zebra stands only 11 to 12 hands. It is also the most startling in appearance, for unlike any other equine, on the throat of both mare and stallion there is a fist-size dewlap with no apparent function. There is yet another striking detail that sets the Mountain Zebra apart from the others and that is the gridiron arrangement of transverse stripes that run down the croup on each side of the median line and across the tail. The rest of the stripe pattern is similar to that of Burchell's Zebra.

The ground color of the coat is white, and the black or brown stripes do not extend to the belly or the insides of the thighs. In conformation, the Mountain Zebra more closely resembles the ass than the horse. Its body is long, its withers very low, and its legs are stocky. The tail is rather scantily haired, but it has a generous tuft. The mane is short, and the finely chiseled head (which is the Mountain Zebra's loveliest feature) is graced by a cinnamon-brown nose and medium-length ears. All told, it presents quite a pleasing picture.

The Mountain Zebra (called *wildeperde*, or wild horse, by the Boers) barely managed to hold its own against the intrepid Boer hunters in the mid-1800's. In the rocky mountains in which it took refuge were large caves, *wildeperde stalle*, which it used for shelter. Inside these caverns it hid from the hunters or bad weather until danger passed and it was safe to venture forth again.

The range of the Mountain Zebra, also known as Hartman's Zebra, is the tip of Africa at the Cape of Good Hope and Angola. But it can now be found only through diligent searching in the less accessible mountain regions where it is presently very strictly protected.

Onager

In a few remote semidesert areas in Asia there exists an animal which appears to be midway between the ass and the horse. Its halfway position seems to have stumped the general public for many years, so that the animal has acquired a variety of names, the most common of which is Onager (pronounced with a hard *g*). Another of the more widely used and revered names (also the most inaccurate) is Mongolian, Persian, or Tibetan Wild Ass. Others, including Kulan, Kiang, and Djiggetai are used in different areas, for it has received a different name in every rural habitat. Scientists settled for the name *Equus hemionus,* and nicknamed it the half-ass, for indeed it does resemble horse and ass equally, half and half. But it really is a species unto itself and breeds true. The Onager constitutes the link between *Equus caballus,* the horse, and *Equus asinus,* the ass.

The Onager is shorter than Przewalski's Horse, standing only 11 to 12 hands at the withers. In the summer it has a red to fawn coat, more or less outlined along the back and around the haunches by a band of white. In winter it is wooly and lighter. The sand-colored coat broken up by the white areas gives the Onager effective camouflage in its desert range. The mane is sparse and upright, black or brown, and the color continues down the back in the form of a very wide dorsal stripe. The tail is tufted like that of the ass, and the hooves are narrow and tough. The ears are most certainly longer than the horse's, but not as long as a donkey's, and the profile of the face varies, on some being straight and on others wavy or sinuous.

For centuries the Onager has lived on the Asian steppes, and

around A.D. 400 it was still seen in eastern parts of Europe. The Mesopotamians caught and tamed it for use in pulling chariots and hauling wagons in about 2500 B.C., as can be seen in drawings of that time. Bas-reliefs also picture Onagers being led about their tasks by the primitive principle of a ring through the nose. This would tend to indicate that the Onager wasn't used as a riding animal, since such a system wouldn't really lend itself to subtle rein guiding from a rider. When horses finally reached the Mediterranean, the use of Onagers was dropped, presumably since the horses were superior draft animals and also ridable. Some scientists have conjectured that Onagers were maintained for some time after the advent of horses for the purpose of producing mules.

Since that early use, the Onager has not been especially desirable to man except as an item of diet or clothing. Its meat is a delicacy, its hide is warm, and its bile is highly regarded in parts of Persia as a sure-fire cure for cataracts. Consequently, its numbers grow fewer and fewer as the years go by. There was once a time when only the most clever strategy and ambush could enable men to catch it, but the gun has very likely doomed it, even in its most remote ranges.

The Onager is sometimes found as high as seven thousand feet in the summer, probably in order to escape civilization. Since it cannot get enough water from forage, it usually drinks daily, so its water supply severely limits its roaming. In the winter, it eats snow and can drift considerably farther.

It lives in groups of five to fifteen, with mares, foals, and one stallion. The foals are swift enough, almost from birth, to keep up with the herd and escape their chief wild enemy, the wolf. This is no mean feat considering that the Onager can go as fast as a race horse, hitting and sustaining speeds of up to thirty-five miles per hour. When they are surprised, they streak for the open plains where they can run unhindered and choose their own directions. They have a tendency to scatter when chased. This is probably a protective device, since if the pursuer hesitates in his choice (which is known to happen) he won't catch any of them. But it is difficult to get close to them initially because they are extremely suspicious and wary, nearly unassailable on the open steppes.

The suspicion, however, is reserved for animals other than themselves. Among their own members they are very sociable. The small herds join together in winter to form groups of up to a thousand (where they are that numerous). There is not such a premium on water holes in winter and a large herd provides protection against cold and predators when activity is curtailed and limited by frigid weather.

The future of *Equus hemione*, the Onager, the half-ass, is uncertain. Hopefully, sufficient restrictions will be placed upon hunting that the species will not become extinct. Some are to be found in zoos in America and other countries.

Przewalski's Horse

THE FIRST ITEM which comes to the fore when people want to discuss Przewalski's Horse is the pronunciation of the name, for it is difficult to sound very intelligent about the subject if the name comes out differently every time. The little Mongolian Wild Horse was named after a Russian explorer to whom the first specimen recognized by science was presented in 1880. So the name is pronounced in the Russian manner — Presh-val'-skee.

Przewalski's Horse, scientifically known as *Equus caballus przewalskii*, is of a different subspecies from the modern domesticated horse, *Equus caballus caballus*, but it is so closely related that it can interbreed with the horse and produce fertile offspring. It is this fact that has led scientists to believe that the ungainly little Mongolian Wild Horse may be the common ancestor of the modern horse, although hundreds or thousands of generations may have passed since the subspecies of *caballus caballus* branched off.

The ability to interbreed with domestic horses very nearly spelled the end of the Wild Horse during the last century, for its range in the highlands of central Asia became more and more crowded as civilization encroached. Domesticated mares provided such temptation to the wild stallions that they not only mated with them, but also abducted them and killed the tame stallions. They ate the haystacks of the Mongolian nomads when winter left them on the edge of starvation, and this was probably the final blow to the herdsmen, who retaliated by going after them with everything at hand, killing them ruthlessly and driving them from their water holes into the desert when summer came, for they knew that without water most of the wild horses would perish within a few days, and this was their goal. They were quite successful over the years. Some of the few ponies that escaped the purge were not pure stock due to crossbreeding, so that by the end of the 1800's there were few true Przewalski's Horses left.

Around the turn of the century, about three dozen foals were captured by Carl Hagenbeck of Germany for menagerie purposes and distributed to several countries, the United States among them. From this nucleus there are now over one hundred Mongolian Wild Horses in captivity, which is very fortunate, for recent expeditions have searched diligently for survivors on the old range at the edge of the Gobi Desert and have found none at all. So Przewalski's Horse may be extinct in the wild state, even though it was still often seen there in 1950. There is a plan afoot to release a colony of stock into a semiwild preserve so that Przewalski's Horse may once more be observed in its feral state. A stud book has been kept since 1902, with careful records and genealogies, a better and longer record than many of the prominent domestic breed registries at this point.

Originally, Przewalski's Horse formed herds of five to fifteen animals, mares and foals under the leadership of a stallion. This is an ancient pattern, very similar to that which the mustangs of the American West adopted after escaping captivity. The Mongolian Ponies were feisty little creatures, standing about 12 hands, with blunt, heavy heads and large bones. Their appearance is still the same today as it apparently was in Pleistocene times, for cave drawings from about that age show horses with the same features, build, and coloring as today's Przewalski's Horse. The color pattern is unique, being a reddish tan fading to white on the belly. The area around its eyes and nose is white, and there is some black below the knees. The mane and tail are auburn to black, and an eel stripe is present although sometimes only very faintly. Przewalski's Horse has been called a dun, but this is not so, for the dun horse never has a mealy nose. In the winter when the coat is thicker, it is often several shades lighter; the mane, which stands up in zebra fashion in the summer, falls to one side or the other from its own weight. The tail is slightly tufted, although not quite as much as an ass's. The pony's head is massive and heavy-jawed in addition to being roman-nosed, and it doesn't have even the saving grace of a forelock to soften the profile, for the mane stops short between the small ears. As might be expected, the Mongolian Wild Horse has good legs and extremely hard hooves, rather small like those of the ass. It has chestnuts on all four legs, as do horses.

In literature, Przewalski's Horse is often mistaken for, or classed indiscriminately with, the Tarpan, another subspecies of wild horse. Its coloring, build, and features are different, though, as well as its range. The Tarpan has been technically extinct for many years, although an attempt is being made to re-create it. Only time will tell whether Przewalski's Horse will follow in the Tarpan's lonely hoofprints.

Tarpan

THE EARLY HISTORY of the Tarpan closely resembles that of the Mongolian Wild Horse, Przewalski's Horse. Both probably came from the same ancestral stock, but their different environments made changes in them. Whereas Przewalski's Horse lived on the dry Asian steppes, the Tarpan lived among the rich, fertile steppes and forests of Russia and Europe. Their differences were obvious. The ancient Tarpans were prettier than the Mongolian Wild Horse. They had more the rounded form of the horse than the angular asslike shape of Przewalski's Horse. Their color was mousy-gray dun, with black legs, nose, and tail. Their legs and inner thighs were sometimes barred, and the entire coat acquired a whitish cast in winter. Down the back ran a black eel stripe, and although the mane appeared silvery from each side, the eel stripe ran down the center of the crest giving an odd two-tone effect. This characteristic is seen today in the Norwegian Fiord Ponies, which seem to be rather pure descendants, as can be deduced from their appearance. The mane stood up like a scrub brush in the summer but often flopped in the winter when it grew thicker and heavier.

The Tarpan's head was unique. It was comparatively light and long, and the profile was what might be called wavy. It was somewhat concave overall, with two slight depressions, one between the eyes and one situated in the lower third of the muzzle. This wavy profile is often seen in the Gotland Horse today. The depression in the forehead caused the eye sockets to protrude above the level of the forehead, giving something of an inquisitive look.

The nose was low and short with bulging nostrils and the ears were longish and pointed.

The peasants went out onto the steppes and captured the wild Tarpans when their stock became depleted, and they prized the ponies for their fine legs and dense hooves. It was this custom of catching and using the wild ponies that made scientists of the 1800's believe that the Tarpans running free were just domestic ponies gone wild. So they made no outcry when the peasants exterminated the ponies because of their depredations on the haystacks and tame horse herds. The last Tarpan was shot in 1880, and shortly after this the Polish authorities became belatedly concerned over the extinction of the species. They gathered up Tarpan-like ponies from the peasants and put them into forest reserves near Bialowieza, Poland, to try to preserve what might be left. The purity of these ponies was questioned, but at least they were closely related and partial descendants of the original Tarpans.

Efforts have been made since the early 1900's at the Hellabrun Zoo in Munich, Germany, to re-create the Tarpan as it was in its wild state long ago. With old descriptions, drawings, and bones and skulls of ancient Tarpans, they set up specific goals. Gathering Przewalski stallions having as many Tarpan characteristics as possible, and using the native Konik mares (from the forest preserves) and Norwegian Fiord mares (since the Norwegian ponies also had a Tarpan-type build, mousy-gray coloring, and the stiff mane with black central stripe), they began a breeding program.

Many years were to pass before the resulting foals began to meet the stringent blueprints set up years before. Even after many ideal Tarpan-like ponies began to appear, it wasn't unusual for throwbacks to occur, and much elimination of imperfect animals was necessary. It must have seemed a hopeless and unending task at times, coupled with the uncertainty of the final results. Now, some fifty years and several generations later, the little reborn Tarpans are breeding true to type and have all the observable characteristics of the original Tarpan, as well as identical skull, bones, teeth, and vertebrae. It is up to the individual as to whether he wants to call this creation a "real Tarpan." There is no way to tell any physical difference, since the end result is a collection of any original blood and the rejection of un-Tarpan-like features. The Tarpan of today might well be more purely Tarpan than some of the last living examples, since they may have had considerable domestic blood in their makeup.

There is conjecture as to what parts the Tarpan and Przewalski's Horse played in forming modern horse breeds. It has been suggested that the Tarpan had a major role in forming the warm-blooded, or light horses, while Przewalski's Horse helped to form the cold-blooded, or draft-type horses. Whatever the case, there was probably considerable admixture so that, except for a few of the northern ponies which seem to be nearly pure Tarpan type, most other horses are very likely a combination of the two parent stocks, and perhaps some other highly debated European ancestors as well. But, no matter how hot and furious the discussion rages (and it often does in scientific and horsey circles), we'll never know for certain.

Zebrorse

IT WOULDN'T be fair to tell about donkeys, ponies, horses, and zebras without a few words about the delightful hybrids the zebra crosses make. The various names are very expressive: a zonkey is naturally the result of a zebra-donkey match, a zeony is the outcome of a zebra-pony mating, and a zebrorse happens when zebra and horse interbreed. There is a bagful of other descriptive terms if you like, including zebrule, zebrula, zebrass, zebra-horse, zebra-mule, zebroid (a combination of the words zebra and hybrid), and horsebra. Whatever the name, the animals aren't very common and are rarely seen, appearing only in captivity.

To breed the zebra to another equine (other than a zebra) calls for quite a bit of diplomacy. As with donkey-horse crosses designed to produce hinnies, the sire must not be allowed to mate with its own species. If the zebra sire, for instance, mates with another zebra, it can never be persuaded to do so with a donkey or horse. Despite precautions, some attempts meet with failure, but in that event, artificial insemination can be successfully used. The work is well worth the trouble, though, for the offspring are colorful, and, if intelligently handled, are quite as lovable as any pony or donkey. The appearance of the animals varies with their breeding.

The zonkey is a captivating creature, usually with white legs and a base color similar to that of his parents. The legs are as heavily striped as the zebra's and there is often a delicate pattern of stripes on the forehead and face. The usual cross on the shoulders is marked with a few fine stripes, and stripes are faint over much of the body. The ears are marked zebra fashion, being white with broad stripes at the base and with black tips. The end of the nose is colored instead of white. The tail is about as full as a mule's, but what really makes the visual difference between the zonkey and a heavily barred donkey is the white upright mane with a black center stripe down its length. In conformation, the zonkey is much like the donkey but with a more rounded body, a heavier neck, and neater proportions.

The zeony and zebrorse are much the same except for size and the fact that the zeony is much more appealing due to its pony features. Its coloring is much the same as the donkey's, the base color being credited to the nonzebra parent. Its conformation seems to approximate a pony or horse's except that the back is straighter, the tail sparser, and the mane often has the black center streak and white sides. The zeony and zebrorse have longer manes than the zebra and a suggestion of a forelock, resembling the Norwegian Fiord Pony in this and in respect to coloration.

There are advantages and disadvantages in the zebra crosses. One major disadvantage is that all offspring are infertile, so the difficult matching must be accomplished anew each time. Another objection is that zonkeys, zeonies, and zebrorses have their own opinions about what should be done, how, why, where, and for how long. When they get tired, it is difficult to make them continue working, whereas a donkey or pony will work a full day without complaint.

While a zeony is reasonably easy to work with, the zonkey has inherited a full complement of stubbornness from both parents. Infinite patience will accomplish good results, but the zebrorse and zeony are much more rewarding to work with. For instance, a zeony is willing and quite strong for its size, a six-hundred-pound zeony pulling the same load that would tax a nine-hundred-pound pony. They can all be broken to ride and drive, and they are dependable to an extent, provided their contrariness is taken into account.

Striping is an interesting phenomenon. Stripes are sometimes seen on purebred horses of established breeds, such as the Connemara Pony, Quarter Horse, and Icelandic Pony, and are found on the legs, sometimes extending a little above the hocks and knees. While this doesn't indicate zebra breeding, it does suggest that perhaps stripes were in the color scheme of the ancestral horse. Buckskins with striped legs are highly prized, and some buckskins have nearly as much striping as a zebrorse or zeony.

Although the zonkey, zebrorse, and zeony are merely exhibition animals now, there was active interest in them in Africa around the first turn of the century, and an attempt was made to create from horse and zebra a hybrid immune to Africa's tsetse fly. It was hoped that the cross would prove stronger and more tractable than the pure zebra. The advent of mechanization put an end to such speculations, and breeding attempts were dropped.

From the standpoint of science and experimentation in such areas as fertilization, genes, and hybridization, it would be interesting to explore this field further with various crosses, colors, and conformations. The information gathered about genetics would be invaluable, and some intriguing questions such as, "What is the result of a zebra-Appaloosa cross?" might have some fascinating answers — dotted lines, perhaps?

Zeony

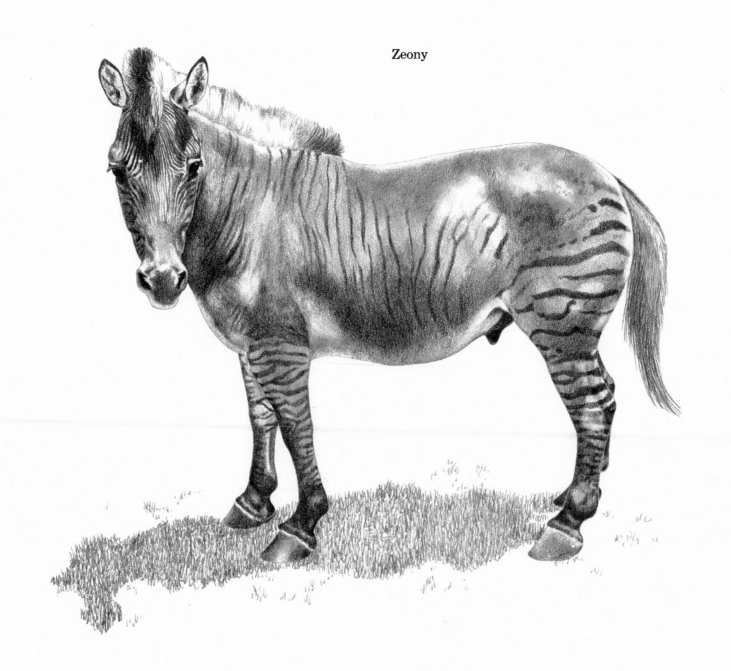

BOOKS

Bailey, Liberty Hyde. *Cyclopedia of American Agriculture.* Vol. III of IV, 1917. 708 pp.

Briggs, Hilton M. *Modern Breeds of Livestock.* rev. ed. New York: Macmillan Co., 1949. 755 pp. ill.

Bruns, Ursula. *Ponies.* Princeton, New Jersey: D. Van Nostrand Co., Inc., 1960. ill.

Denhardt, Robert M. *The Horse of the Americas.* Norman: University of Oklahoma Press, 1948. 286 pp.

Dillon, Richard H. *Meriwether Lewis.* New York: Coward-McCann, Inc., 1965. 364 pp. ill.

Disston, Harry. *Know About Horses.* New York: Devin-Adair Co., 1961. ill.

Dobie, J. Frank. *The Mustangs.* New York: Bantam Books, Inc., 1954. 304 pp.

Fox, Charles Phillip. *A Pictorial History of Performing Horses.* Seattle: Superior Publishing Co., 1960. 168 pp. ill.

Goodall, Daphne Machin. *Horses of the World.* New York: Macmillan Co., 1965.

Gorman, John A. *The Western Horse.* 4th ed. Danville, Ill.: Interstate Printers and Publishers, Inc., 1958. 445 pp.

Griffen, Jeff. *The Pony Book.* New York: Doubleday & Co., Inc., 1966.

Haines, Frances. *Appaloosa, the Spotted Horse in Art and History.* Austin, Tex.: University of Texas Press, 1963. 103 pp. ill.

Hamlyn, Paul. *Horses, Horses, Horses.* London: Paul Hamlyn Ltd., 1962. 152 pp. ill.

Hayes, Captain H. M. *The Points of the Horse.* London: W. Thacker and Co., 1893. 378 pp. ill.

Henry, Marguerite. *Album of Horses.* Chicago: Rand McNally & Co., 1951. ill.

"Horse." *Encyclopedia Americana.* Vol. 14. 1967. 386–402.

"Horse." *Encyclopedia Britannica.* Vol. 11. 1969. 701–707.

Howard, Robert West. *The Horse in America.* Chicago: Follett Publishing Co., 1965. 298 pp. ill.

Kays, Donald J. *The Horse.* Cranbury, New Jersey: New York: Barnes, A. S. & Co., 1953. ill.

Mitchell, Ehrman B. *Ponies for Young People.* Princeton, New Jersey: D. Van Nostrand Co., 1960. ill.

Muybridge, Eadweard. *Animals in Motion.* New York: Dover Publications, Inc., 1957. 416 pp. 4000 photographs.

Olson, Everett C. *The Evolution of Life.* London: Weidenfield & Nicolson, 1965. 300 pp. ill.

Olson, Everett C. "Horse." *Colliers Encyclopedia.* Vol. 12. 1967. 252–263.

Plumb, Charles S. *Types and Breeds of Farm Animals.* Boston: Ginn & Co., 1906. 563 pp. ill.

Sanderson, Ivan T. *Living Mammals of the World.* Garden City, New York: Hanover House, 1955. 303 pp.

Shaw, Thomas. *Animal Breeding.* Chicago: Orange Judd Co., 1911. 406 pp.

Simpson, George Gaylord. *Horses.* New York: Doubleday & Co., Inc., 1961. 323 pp.

Summerhays, R. S. *The Observer's Book of Horses & Ponies.* rev. ed. New York: Frederick Warne & Co., Inc., 1968. 267 pp.

Taylor, Louis. *The Horse America Made.* Evanston, Ill.: Harper & Row, 1961. 250 pp. ill.

Thayer, Bert C. *The Thoroughbred.* New York: Meredith Press, 1964. ill.

Vaughan, Henry W. *Types and Market Classes of Livestock.* Columbus: R. G. Adams & Co., 1934.

Wynmalen, Henry. *Horse Breeding and Stud Management.* Hackensack, New Jersey: Wehman Bros., 1964.

Zeuner, Friedrich E. *A History of Domesticated Animals.* Evanston, Ill.: Harper & Row, 1964. ill.

MAGAZINES

Castle, Dr. W. E., and F. L. King. "The Albino in Palomino Breeding." *The Western Horseman,* reprint from November-December issues, 1947.

Estes, Richard D. "Trials of a Zebra Herd Stallion." *Natural History.* Vol. 76, No. 9 (November, 1967).

Hildebrand, Milton. "Symmetrical Gaits of Horses." *Science.* Vol. 150, No. 3697 (November 5, 1965).

Martin, Paul S. "Pleistocene Overkill." *Natural History.* Vol. 76, No. 10 (December, 1967).

Willoughby, David P. "The Vanished Quagga." *Natural History.* Vol. 75, No. 2 (February, 1966).

The Western Horseman. Numerous articles from issues between January, 1965, and August, 1968; some issues from other years.